PONTYPRIDD
TO
PORT TALBOT

Vic Mitchell and Keith Smith

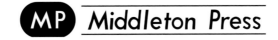
MP *Middleton Press*

Front cover: It is 26th July 1958 and one of the new class 115 DMUs waits by the old carriage shed at the end of the branch, at Maerdy. Coal sidings are in the background. (G.Adams/M.J.Stretton coll.)

Back cover upper: Treherbert trains pass at Porth on 29th January 1979. The platforms are in the background and the Maerdy branch is on the left. (P.Jones)

Back cover lower: We are at Pontypridd on 17th August 1981. Nos 37282 and 37305 pause alongside the retaining wall with an empty Merry-go-Round train, while no. 37280 waits on the down relief line with a ballast train. (P.Jones)

Published October 2010

ISBN 978 1 906008 86 4

© Middleton Press, 2010

Design Deborah Esher

Published by
Middleton Press
Easebourne Lane
Midhurst
West Sussex
GU29 9AZ
Tel: 01730 813169
Fax: 01730 812601
Email: info@middletonpress.co.uk
www.middletonpress.co.uk

Printed in the United Kingdom by Henry Ling Limited, at the Dorset Press, Dorchester, DT1 1HD

INDEX

ACKNOWLEDGEMENTS

We are very grateful for the assistance received from many of those mentioned in the credits also to A.R.Carder, R.Caston, L.Crosier, G.Croughton, T.Hancock, S.C.Jenkins, N.Langridge, B.Lewis, D.H.Mitchell, D.T.Rowe, Mr D. and Dr S.Salter, N.W.Sprinks, S.Vincent, T.Walsh and in particular, our always supportive wives, Barbara Mitchell and Janet Smith.

Postscript: as this volume was about to go to the printers, we heard of the death of Larry Crosier, a devoted student of GWR signalling. This is a great loss to his many admirers.

I. GWR map for 1937.

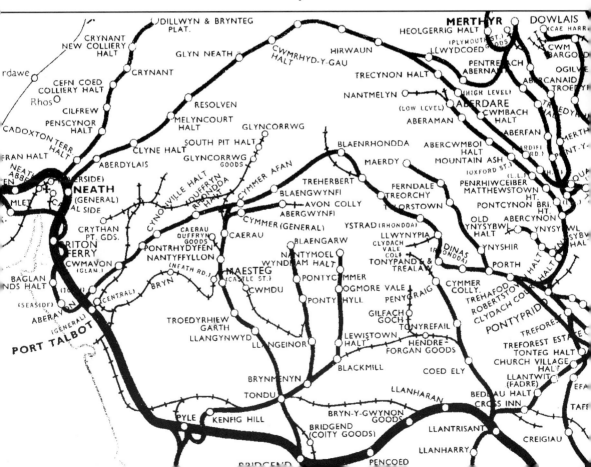

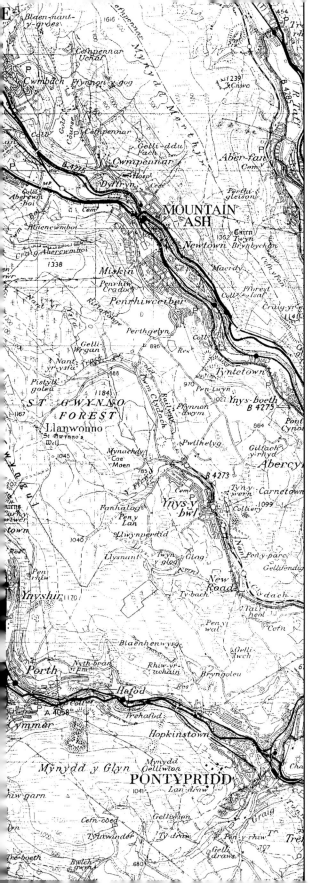

GEOGRAPHICAL SETTING

While one travels up most Glamorganshire valleys in a northerly direction, those at the west end of the group involve a journey northwest. We start in the Taff Vale at Pontypridd and enter the Rhondda Valley. After 2½ miles, it divides at Porth into the Rhondda Fach, which runs up to Maerdy, and the Rhondda Fawr, which is urbanised over a greater length. Ystrad Rhondda is near its midpoint and Blaenrhondda is at its upper end. Both valleys have been intensively worked for coal; there were 53 pits in 1913 for example. None now exist and most evidence has gone.

A turn west at the head of the valley takes us through the remarkable Rhondda Tunnel into the head of the Avan Valley, once a site of further intensive coal mining. A ten mile descent along this now attractive incision in the uplands brings us to a still industrialised area around Port Talbot. While there are docks here now as a result of the development of the steel industry, in the late 19th century most coal for export continued west to the docks at Swansea. The human cost was enormous at that time, with a Rhondda miner killed every six hours and one injured every two minutes, on average.

The maps are to the scale of 25ins to 1 mile, 1920 edition, with north at the top unless otherwise indicated. Welsh spelling and hyphenation has varied over the years and so we have generally used the form used by the railways at the time.

II.   1954 edition at 1ins to 1 mile. Maerdy is above centre on the left page and Treherbert is to the left of it.

HISTORICAL BACKGROUND

The South Wales Railway opened through Cardiff to Swansea in 1850 and became part of the Great Western Railway in 1863. The Taff Vale Railway had predated this by coming into use between Cardiff, Pontypridd and Abercynon on 9th October 1840. Its Act was dated 21st June 1836. The engineer for both railways was I.K.Brunel, but he specified the SWR to be broad gauge and TVR as standard. (The former was converted in 1872). The latter was provided with a branch west to Trehafod in June 1841 and it was extended northwards to Ynyshir and westwards to Dinas in 1849. The Ynyshir branch was extended to Ferndale in 1856 and to Maerdy in 1886. The route beyond Dinas was opened to the Blaenrhondda district in 1856.

While passengers were carried on the SWR from the outset, the TVR waited until 7th August 1863 to offer this service to Treherbert. The Maerdy branch followed to Ferndale on 5th June 1876 and to Maerdy itself on 18th June 1889.

The remainder of our route developed generally west-east from Port Talbot. The Rhondda & Swansea Bay Railway was incorporated in 1882 and was planned as a means of providing an alternative route to the coast for coal from the Rhondda Valley. The Swansea Docks to Port Talbot section was built close to the coast and opened in 1893-94. The middle section, between Port Talbot (Aberavon) and Cymmer was built partially on the site of the Cwmafan Railway and was opened on 25th June 1885 to Pontrhydyfen and on 2nd November following to Cymmer. Trains began running through the long Rhondda Tunnel to Blaenrhondda on 2nd July 1890. They continued to Treherbert two weeks later. The middle and eastern sections carried passengers from the dates stated.

The South Wales Mineral Railway came into use in 1861-63 and carried passengers between Cymmer and Glyncorrwg in 1918-30. It became part of the GWR in 1922, along with the R&SBR.

The Llynvi & Ogmore Railway began operating in 1866 on part of the 1861 Llynvi Valley Railway and was completed through Cymmer Tunnel to Cymmer in 1878. It was incorporated into the GWR in 1883. It carried passengers south from Cymmer from 1878 to 1970. The line was broad gauge initially, mixed gauge from 1863 and standard only from 1872. It was extended east to Abergwynfi in 1878 and passenger services were provided from 1886 until 1960, when a new link was laid to divert trains to Blaengwynfi instead.

The GWR became the Western Region of British Railways upon nationalisation in 1948. Passenger service was withdrawn between Cymmer and Aberavon (Town) on 3rd December 1962 and between Treherbert and Cymmer on 26th February 1968, following the closure of Rhondda Tunnel on safety grounds. The Maerdy branch closed on 15th June 1964, but the Cardiff-Pontypridd-Treherbert service continues. Freight withdrawals are given in the captions. Track singling took place between Treherbert and Treorchy in 1972 and on to Porth in 1981.

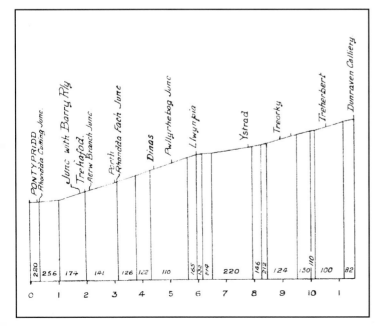

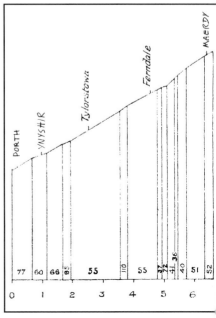

PASSENGER SERVICES

Pontypridd-Treherbert

The table right shows the number of trains to Treherbert and most of them started at Cardiff.

	Weekdays	Sundays
1869	4	2
1882	5	2
1892	8	2
1920	17	4
1950	25	9
1983	19	8
2010	31	7

Maerdy Branch

The initial service to Ferndale comprised four trains, weekdays only, with two extras on Wednesdays. The 1892 timetable to Maerdy showed figures of 6 (2). The number in brackets refers to Sundays. In 1920, the service was 15 (4), most starting at Pontypridd.

The figures for 1950 were 20 (11), with three extra on Saturdays. The final timetable offered seven weekday trains, with eight more on Saturdays and none on Sundays. Branch trains started at Porth for many years.

West of Treherbert

The initial service offered had six weekday and two Sunday trains. In 1920, the figures were 7 (0) and by 1950 they were 9 (0). Trains were diverted at Cymmer to terminate at Bridgend from December 1962 and eight weekday trains were provided.

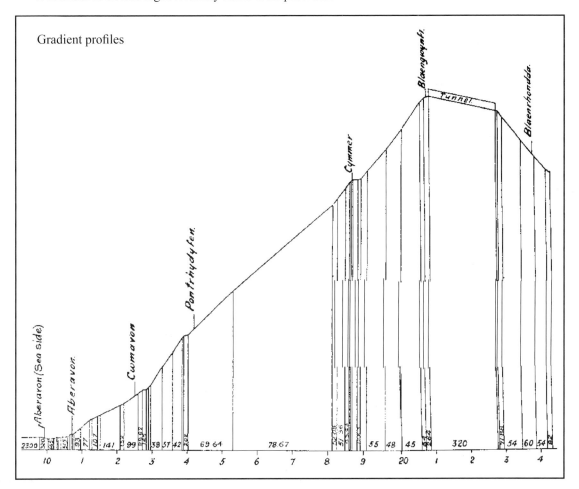

Gradient profiles

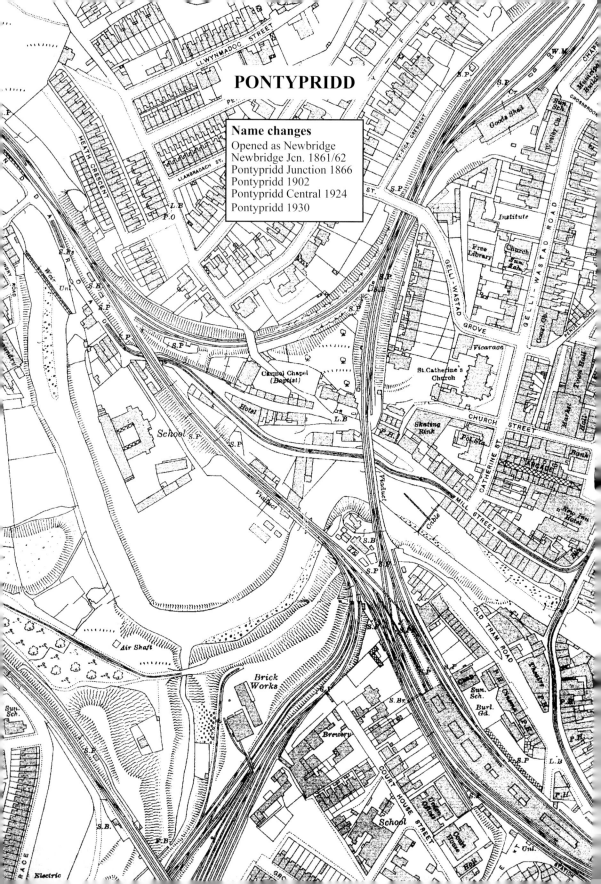

PONTYPRIDD

Name changes
Opened as Newbridge
Newbridge Jcn. 1861/62
Pontypridd Junction 1866
Pontypridd 1902
Pontypridd Central 1924
Pontypridd 1930

← III. The 1919 map at 20ins to 1 mile has the 1840 route of the TVR from Cardiff to Merthyr curving from bottom to top on the right. Until 1860, the Rhondda line branched left north of the viaduct, only one boundary remaining as evidence. The subsequent route diverges at a smaller angle and passes over a viaduct a little upstream of the original. The curve linking the two routes was in use from 1872 until 1968 and at its western end was Rhondda Cutting signal box, which lasted until 16th June 1970. The extent of the station roof is evident lower right and running diagonally lower left is part of the Barry Railway. Between these are sidings serving Maritime Colliery, Penyrhiw Colliery, a brickworks and a brewery. The final disconnection was made in 1968. The complex junction was simplified in 1969-70, leaving only the western platform and a bay at the south end in use. The latter lasted until November 1980. Old Tram Road marks the site of the Thomas Tramroad, a length of which remains on the left of the page. The street tramway is included.

1.   The station was totally rebuilt in 1906-07 and this postcard dates from soon after. The original had two through platforms and can be seen in picture 5.21 in *Brunel - A Railtour of His Achievements* (Middleton Press 2007). The Merthyr Viaduct is in the vicinity of the cloud of steam and the cattle pens are in the foreground. The first rebuilding was in 1891. (Lens of Sutton coll.)

2.   We are at the north end of the station in June 1922, between the bay platforms which were numbered 3 and 4. The through platforms were 1 and 6, with 2, 5 and 7 as long bays within them. In the centre background is the 1902 Junction box. The railings of Rhondda Viaduct (112yds) are on the left and those of Merthyr Viaduct (90yds) on the right. (D.K.Jones coll.)

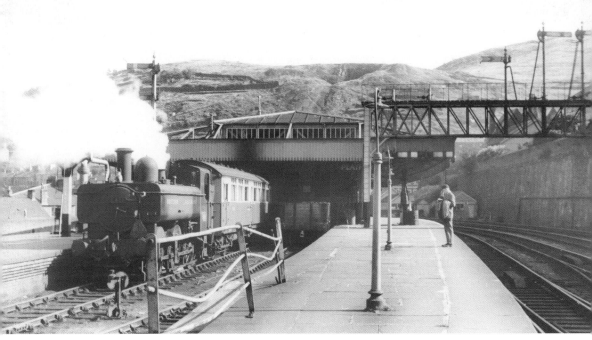

3.   We are still at the north end of the station, but on 11th September 1951 and find 0-6-0PT no. 6411 at platform 4, with an autocoach for Ynysybwl. On the right are two through goods lines, which were designated "relief lines" in October 1988. Staff numbered 154 in 1923 and 119 in 1933, but these figures included train crews. (H.C.Casserley)

4.   A Treherbert to Barry Island train is behind a 2-6-2T in 1956. The engine is crossing the lines to Merthyr. The buffers on the right are on Chapel Siding. The station was called "Central" from 1924 until 1930, when "Graig" station on the former Barry line closed. (D.K.Jones coll.)

5.   The main entrance faces northeast and is at a busy road junction. The TVR crest was added following rebuilding and creation of a new booking hall in 1975. (D.A.Thompson)

6.   A DMU from Treherbert passes over the revised track layout on 24th March 1976, bound for Cardiff General. In the background is the commencement of the Rhondda Valley and also Junction box, which closed on 15th October 1998, after which time the area was controlled from Radyr. (T.Heavyside)

7.   Running south on 8th May 1977 is no. 37279 with coal from Ty Mawr Colliery, bound for Radyr Yard. The siding on the left was used by the engineers after the cessation of cattle traffic in the mid-1960s. Platform 7 had occupied the indent on the right and beyond it was the long platform 6. (P.Jones)

8.   The train on the right is departing for Treherbert on 13th February 2009 and is passing the site of the track for the former platform 2. The platform on the left was opened on the up relief line on 16th September 1991 and numbered 2. It could take four cars, while No. 1 takes 12. (V.Mitchell)

WEST OF PONTYPRIDD

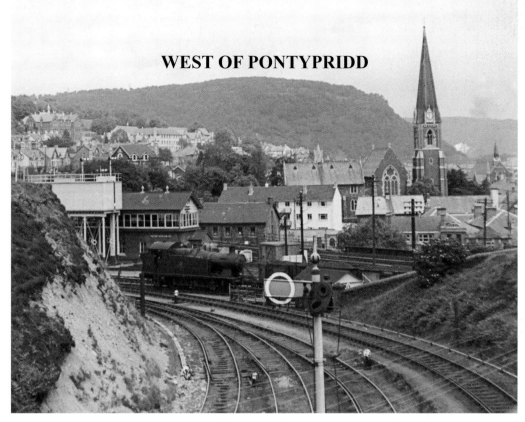

9.   We look north from the centre of the next picture, over the Maritime Colliery sidings, on 15th June 1956. Beyond the class 5600 0-6-2T is Junction box, which had a 135 lever frame. This was shortened to 70 levers in 1970. (J&J coll.)

10.   Wagons are standing on the Maritime Sidings on 26th June 1960 and the Rhondda lines run across the picture. The bridges once spanned the Thomas Tramroad. The tall chimneys are on the brewery, which had its own siding from 1899 until 1933. (M.Dart/Transport Treasury)

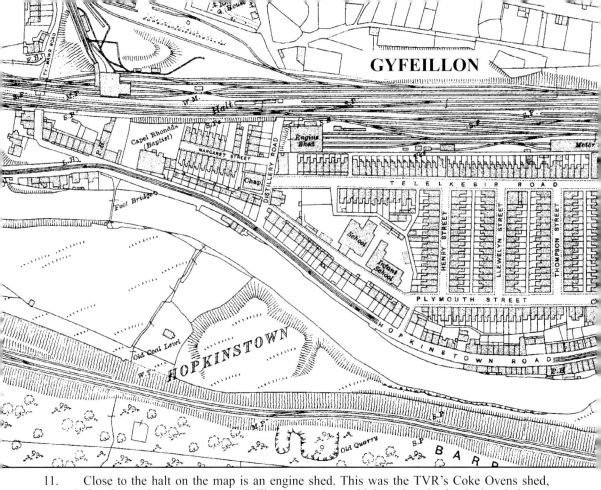

GYFEILLON

11.   Close to the halt on the map is an engine shed. This was the TVR's Coke Ovens shed, named after the nearby Great Western Colliery's premises, which made coke for the iron industry. The shed was open from 1896 to 1933 and is seen in about 1929. It had 40 tank engines allocated in 1926. (LGRP)

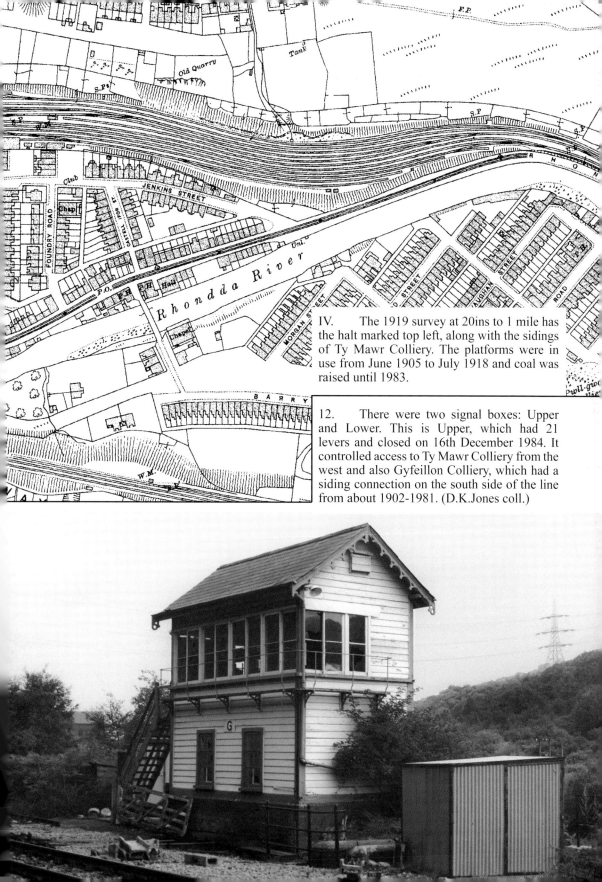

IV. The 1919 survey at 20ins to 1 mile has the halt marked top left, along with the sidings of Ty Mawr Colliery. The platforms were in use from June 1905 to July 1918 and coal was raised until 1983.

12. There were two signal boxes: Upper and Lower. This is Upper, which had 21 levers and closed on 16th December 1984. It controlled access to Ty Mawr Colliery from the west and also Gyfeillon Colliery, which had a siding connection on the south side of the line from about 1902-1981. (D.K.Jones coll.)

13.   A Cardiff to Treherbert DMU passes the site of the halt on 23rd May 1973. Peckett no. 1676 of 1925 is fly shunting with a rope on dreadful track. (T.Heavyside)

EAST OF TREHAFOD

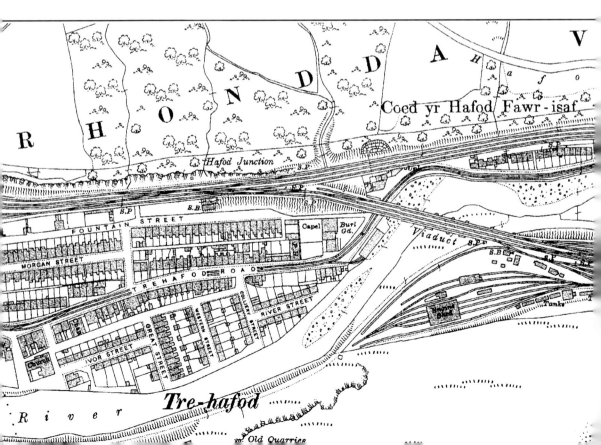

Sec., John Jones, Cardiff.   Gen. Man., A. Beasley.

August 1892

Fares from Cardiff (Queen St.)	Up.	Week Days			Sundys
Cardiff Docks......dep.					
Cardiff (Queen St.) arr.					
Penarth......dep.					
Cardiff (G. W.) "					
Cardiff (Queen St.) dep.					
Llandaff					
Radyr ...					
Walnut Tree Bridge..					
Cowbridge ...dep.					
Ystradowen					
Llanharry					
Llantrissant { arr.					
50, 52 { dep.					
Cross Inn ...					
Llantwit					
Church Village..					
Treforest					
Pontypridd Junction					
Pontypridd Junc. dep.					
Hafod ...					
Porth ...					
Porth ...dep.					
Ynishir					
Tylors Town					
Ferndale					
Maerdy ... arr.					
Dinas					
Llwynypia					
Ystrad					
Treorchy					
Treherbert ... arr.					
Ynysybwl ...dep.					
Aberdare Jun. arr.					
Aberdare Junction 57					
Aberdare Jun. dep.					
Penrhiwceiber					
Mountain Ash					
Aberaman					
Aberdare 44. arr.					
Quaker's Yd. Jn. 46, 276					
Merthyr Vale...					
Troedyrhiew					
Pentrebach					
Merthyr 144, 271, 275					

CADOXTON, PENARTH, and CARDIFF.—Taff Vale.

V.   We continue on the same scale and edition for four pages and have the 1889 Barry Railway coming in lower right. It had built extensive docks at Barry and was a major competitor to the TVR for coal for export. Its engine shed and junction are on the left page. The tracks continue on the right of the next pair of pages, where Trehafod station is shown. The line to Barry was closed in 1951 and the last part removed in 1958, but the engine shed had closed back in 1925.

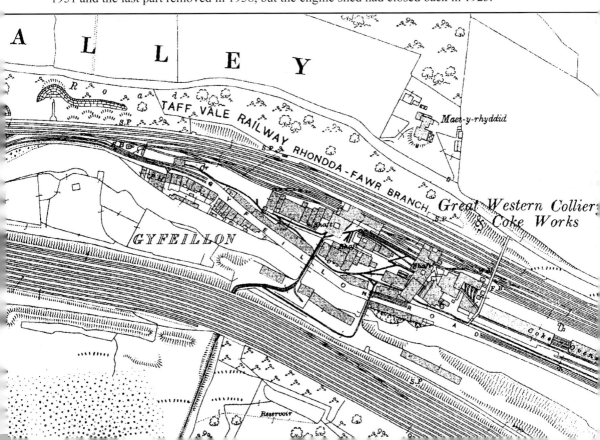

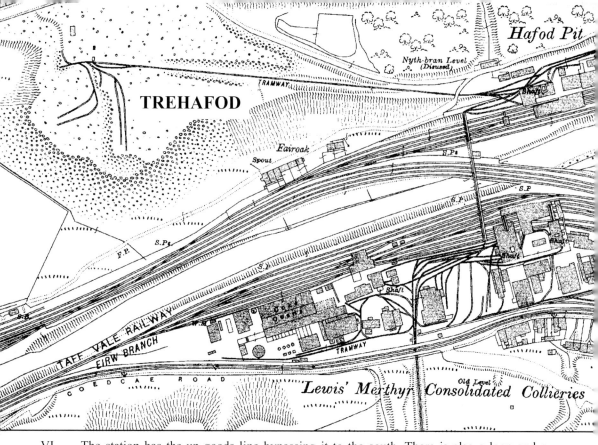

TREHAFOD

Hafod Pit

Nyth-bran Level
(Disused)

Fairoak
Spout

TAFF VALE RAILWAY
EIRW BRANCH

COEDCAE ROAD

Lewis' Merthyr Consolidated Collieries

Old Level

VI.   The station has the up goods line bypassing it to the south. There is also a loop and a short siding, which served as a goods yard until 7th October 1963. These were taken out of use in February 1964. The station opened on 17th October 1892; its predecessor was simply "Hafod" and was below that word. It opened in 1861 and initially Eirw Junction was to the west of it, near the join of the pages. The branch from it was in use from 1854 until 1977. The last colliery served was

14.   A coal train occupies the down goods line in June 1922. The six posts on the left carry signals relating to Trehafod Barry Junction. Only one tree is evident on the barren hills to the south. There was a staff of 31 to 35 in the 1930s. (D.K.Jones coll.)

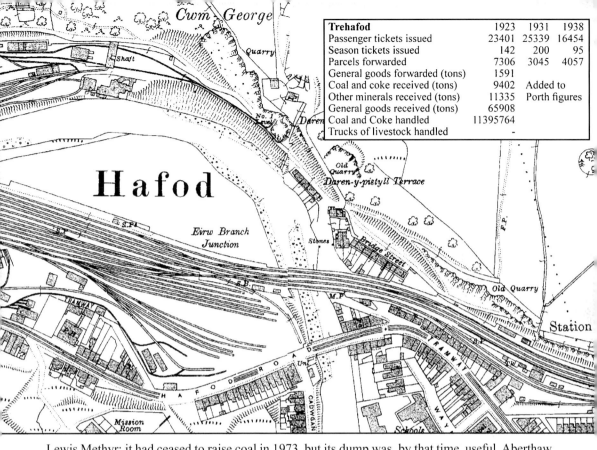

Lewis Methyr; it had ceased to raise coal in 1973, but its dump was, by that time, useful. Aberthaw power station can burn low grade dust, for example. Eirw branch was ¾ mile long and served Cymmer Colliery (at its west end) until 1939 and Porth Gasworks until January 1953. The signal box on the left is Llwyncelin (1907-51); it had 53 levers.

15.   A view up the valley in 1958 includes the signal for the up goods line on the left. Initially Havod, the name became Hafod in November 1890 and Trehafod on 1st January 1905. The colliery buildings on the left have been preserved and are where one may gain an understanding of all the problems of coal mining. See caption 18. (Stations UK)

16. Looking in the same direction on 13th February 2009, we can note the shelter from the 1970s and that a road has been built on the site of the up goods line. The intoxicated passengers had joined the train at Pontypridd at 09.34, destined for a football match in Cardiff. They were now totally lost. (V.Mitchell)

August 1892

PORT TALBOT DOCKS, CYMMER, and TREHERBERT.—Rhondda and Swansea Bay.

High Street,	mrn	mrn	mrn	mrn	aft	aft	aft	aft	aft	aft (Sats. only)		SUNDAYS mrn	aft
SWANSEA 52 ....dep.	....	6 50	8 30	11 0	....	1 30	2 45	3 55	7 25		....	5 55	1240
NEATH 52........ "	....	7 11	8 52	1130	....	2 13	3 6	4 25	7 54		....	6 24	1 13
PORT TALBOT 52. arr.	....	7 28	9 5	1145	....	2 30	3 18	4 44	8 7		....	6 37	1 29
Port Talbot Docks ..dep.	....	....	9 0	....	1 5	....	3 50	6 5	8 15		....	....	....
Aberavon .... arr.	....	....	9 4	....	1 10	....	3 55	6 9	8 20		....	....	....
Aberavon .... dep.	6 0	7 55	9 25	12 5	....	3 40	....	6 20	8 30	10 0	....	9 0	5 0
Cwmavon	6 6	8 1	9 31	1211	....	3 46	....	6 26	8 36	10 5	....	9 6	5 6
Pontrhydyfen	6 13	8 8	9 37	1218	....	3 53	....	6 33	8 43	....	....	9 12	5 12
Cymmer * 55..........	6 24	8 21	9 53	1230	....	4 5	....	6 44	8 54	....	....	9 23	5 23
Blaen-Gwynfy	6 31	8 28	9 59	1236	....	4 11	....	6 52	9 0	....	....	9 29	5 29
Blaen-Rhondda..........	6 38	8 37	10 5	1244	....	4 19	....	7 2	9 8	....	....	9 37	5 37
Treherbert (Taff Vale) ar	....	8 40	10 8	1247	....	4 22	....	7 5	9 11	....	....	9 40	5 40

Down.	mrn	mrn	aft	aft	aft	aft	aft	aft (Sats. only)	SUNDAYS mrn	aft	
Treherbert (Taff Vale) dp	8 3	9 31	1213	2 50	....	6 0	7 20		1015	6 0	....
Blaen-Rhondda	8 6	9 34	1216	2 53	....	6 3	7 23		1019	6 4	....
Blaen-Gwynfy	8 14	9 41	1224	3 1	....	6 11	7 31		1027	6 12	....
Cymmer *	8 21	9 53	1230	3 7	....	6 17	7 37		1033	6 18	....
Pontrhydyfen	8 33	10 6	1241	3 18	....	6 33	7 48		1044	6 29	....
Cwmavon	8 40	1013	1248	3 25	....	6 40	7 54	1025	1050	6 35	....
Aberavon .... arr.	8 45	1018	1253	3 30	....	6 45	7 59	1030	1055	6 40	....
Aberavon .... dep.	8 46	....	1255	3 33	5 50	....	8 5	....	....	....	....
Port Talbot Docks..arr.	8 50	....	1259	3 37	5 54	....	8 10	....	....	....	....
PORT TALBOT 50 dep.	9 1	1120	2 57	4 55	....	7 28	1110	1110	....	7 11	....
NEATH 50.......arr.	9 18	1132	3 16	5 8	....	7 44	1122	1122	....	7 29	....
SWANSEA 50 .... "	9 55	12 0	3 50	5 35	....	8 15	1150	1150	....	8 10	....

* Station for Glyncorrwg.

June 1920

SWANSEA, COURT SART, PORT TALBOT, and TREHERBERT.—Rhondda and Swansea Bay.

Gen. Man., John David, Swansea.

Miles.	**Down.**	Week Days. mrn		mrn	aft	aft (Saturdays only)	aft		aft	aft	aft (Saturdays only)								Suns. mrn	aft
	Treherbert (Taff Vale)..dep.	7 55	....	9 25	1210	....	2 25	....	5 29	7 16	9 10	....	....	....	....	....	....	....	....	....
¾	Blaen-Rhondda	7 58	....	9 29	1214	....	2 28	....	5 33	7 19	9 13	....	....	....	....	....	....	....	....	....
3¼	**Blaengwynfy**	8 9	....	9 40	1222	2 23	2 38	....	5 43	7 29	9 23	....	....	....	....	....	....	....	8 20	5 3
6	Cymmer ¶ 77 *and below* arr.	8 14	....	9 45	1227	2 28	2 43	....	5 48	7 34	9 28	....	....	....	....	....	....	....	8 25	5 8
	Cymmer dep.	8 15	....	9 47	1229	2 30	2 44	....	5 56	7 35	9 29	....	....	....	....	....	....	....	8 26	5 9
10¼	Pontrhydyfen	8 29	....	9 58	1245	2 45	2 58	....	6 7	7 48	9 42	....	....	....	....	....	....	....	8 40	5 24
12	Cwmavon	8 36	....	10 5	1252	2 52	3 5	....	6 14	7 55	9 49	....	....	....	....	....	....	....	8 47	5 31
13½	Port Talbot (Aberavon) *(below)* arr.	8 41	....	1010	1257	2 57	3 10	....	6 19	8 0	9 54	....	....	....	....	....	....	....	8 53	5 37
	Port Talbot dep.	8 42	....	1012	1259	3 0	3 12	....	6 21	8 3	9 55	....	....	....	....	....	....	....	....	....
14¾	**Aberavon (Seaside)**........	8 45	....	1016	1 3	3 4	3 17	....	6 25	8 s 6	....	....	....	....	....	....	....	....	....	....
17½	Briton Ferry **44, 48**	8 52	....	1023	1 11	3 10	3 24	....	6 32	8 12	10 5	....	....	....	....	....	....	....	....	....
18½	Court Sart *(below)* .... arr.	8 54	....	1025	1 13	3 12	3 26	....	6 34	8 14	10 7	....	....	....	....	....	....	....	....	....
	Court Sart dep.	8 55	....	1026	1 15	3 14	3 27	....	6 36	8 16	10 9	....	....	....	....	....	....	....	....	....
21¼	**Jersey Marine**..............	9 3	....	1034	1 22	3 22	3 35	....	6 44	8 24	1019	....	....	....	....	....	....	....	....	....
23¼	**Danygraig**	9 11	....	1043	1 32	3 30	3 44	....	6 51	8 33	....	....	....	....	....	....	....	....	....	....
24¼	**Swansea 373, 497**......arr.	9 16	....	1046	1 35	3 33	3 49	....	6 55	8 38	1030	....	....	....	....	....	....	....	....	....

s Saturdays only.

¶ "**Halts**" at Cynonville and Duffryn Rhondda, between Pontrhydyfen and Cymmer.

WEST OF TREHAFOD

17.   Work started at Lewis Merthyr Colliery back in 1850. Later W.T.Lewis became Lord Merthyr and applied both his names. Trefor shaft was in use from 1878 to 1958 and Bertie shaft from 1890 to 1960. There were 24 miles of underground railways covering 12 square miles. The Eirw branch is on the far bank of the river. (Lens of Sutton coll.)

18.   The four tracks of the previous picture have become two and one shaft has been lost, as have the cottages. The date is 25th March 1976 and no. 37227 has just passed the Porth distant signal. The Rhondda Heritage Park was begun on the site in the background in 1989 and has now an outstanding collection of working machinery. A visit is essential for those interested in the district. (T.Heavyside)

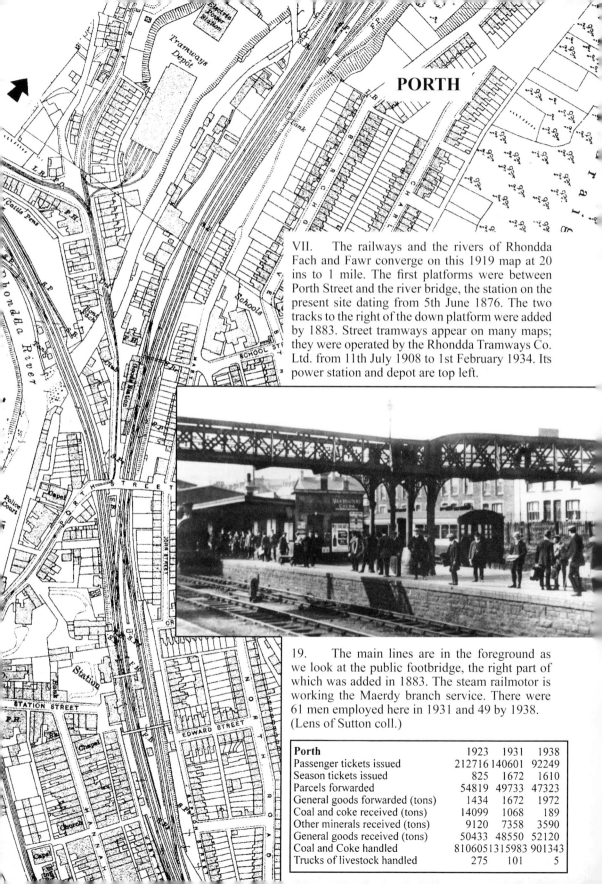

VII.   The railways and the rivers of Rhondda Fach and Fawr converge on this 1919 map at 20 ins to 1 mile. The first platforms were between Porth Street and the river bridge, the station on the present site dating from 5th June 1876. The two tracks to the right of the down platform were added by 1883. Street tramways appear on many maps; they were operated by the Rhondda Tramways Co. Ltd. from 11th July 1908 to 1st February 1934. Its power station and depot are top left.

19.   The main lines are in the foreground as we look at the public footbridge, the right part of which was added in 1883. The steam railmotor is working the Maerdy branch service. There were 61 men employed here in 1931 and 49 by 1938. (Lens of Sutton coll.)

Porth	1923	1931	1938
Passenger tickets issued	212716	140601	92249
Season tickets issued	825	1672	1610
Parcels forwarded	54819	49733	47323
General goods forwarded (tons)	1434	1672	1972
Coal and coke received (tons)	14099	1068	189
Other minerals received (tons)	9120	7358	3590
General goods received (tons)	50433	48550	52120
Coal and Coke handled	810605	1315983	901343
Trucks of livestock handled	275	101	5

20.   A panorama down the valley features two goods lines and three for passengers. The short siding could be used by railmotors between trips. The route from Trehafod had been doubled in 1860; Dinas followed in 1861. (D.K.Jones coll.)

21.   The 1861 platforms were beyond the bridge on the left and served as the passenger terminus for two years. The unusual tapered signal box is seen on 17th August 1963 and was in use until 27th March 1966. It was called Rhonddach Fach Junction North and had 115 levers. (P.J.Garland/R.S.Carpenter coll.)

22.   Seen on the same day from a DMU from Maerdy is the goods yard, which was open until 7th September 1964. It was provided with a 10-ton crane. (P.J.Garland/R.S.Carpenter coll.)

23.   We are near the bottom edge of the map, with the station and public footbridge in the background. No. 37275 is working from Maerdy Colliery to Aberaman Phurnacite Plant on 25th March 1976. South box is out of view, on the left. Its 75-lever frame was in use until 29th March 1981. (T.Heavyside)

24.   The route onwards was singled on 29th March 1981 and so the 14.00 Barry Island to Treherbert has just used the new crossover on 29th June 1981. It is obscuring the new connection for the Maerdy branch. A long inclined footway now occupies the space on the right. (T.Heavyside)

25.   A view in the other direction in 1984 includes the 1981 signal box at the end of the up platform. It housed 16 levers and closed on 15th October 1998. On the left is part of the 100ft long mural created by local school pupils in 1979. (D.K.Jones coll.)

Maerdy Branch
YNYSHIR

26.   This 1922 view up the valley has an island platform beyond the bridge. The station opened as Ynishir in 1885 and became Ynyshir in 1907. It is often spoken Un-us-here. The line was doubled in 1876, trebled in 1888 and singled in 1966. (D.K.Jones coll.)

27.   This view of the ticket office is from about 1950; it is also on the bridge in the previous picture. Ynyshir signal box had 66 levers and was in use from 1st July 1934 until 14th June 1964. There were 28 men to cover here and Wattstown in 1923, the figure dropping to 12 in 1933. (Lens of Sutton coll.)

28.   A photograph from a down DMU on 17th August 1963 includes Lady Lewis Colliery, the sidings for which were in use in 1903-64. Aber Rhondda Colliery had a connection on the other side of the valley until 1906. North of the station, there were sidings on the west side for Ynyshir Standard Colliery in 1931-62. One totem nameboard indicates that the station is still open. (P.J.Garland/R.S.Carpenter coll.)

WATTSTOWN PLATFORM

29.   A northward postcard view features the goods yard, which was closed on 7th October 1963. The platforms were to the left of the camera and were in use from 5th June 1906 until 12th July 1920. Behind us and to the right was Wattstown National Colliery, which had sidings from 1904 until 1970, although it closed on 22nd November 1968. (Lens of Sutton coll.)

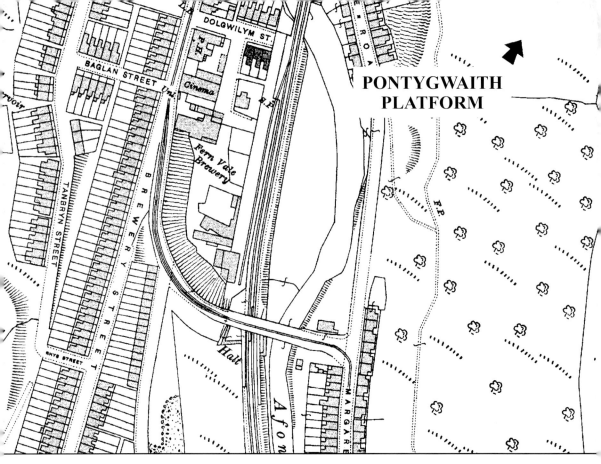

PONTYGWAITH PLATFORM

VIII.   This was open from 5th June 1906 until 1st October 1914. There was a siding on the up side from 1894 until 1963; it was used for various commercial purposes. The steps to the platforms still had roofs by the time of the 1920 survey.

30.   This damaged postcard view is from the hillside on the east of the valley. The buildings on the right of the bridge are adjacent to the siding. (A.Dudman coll.)

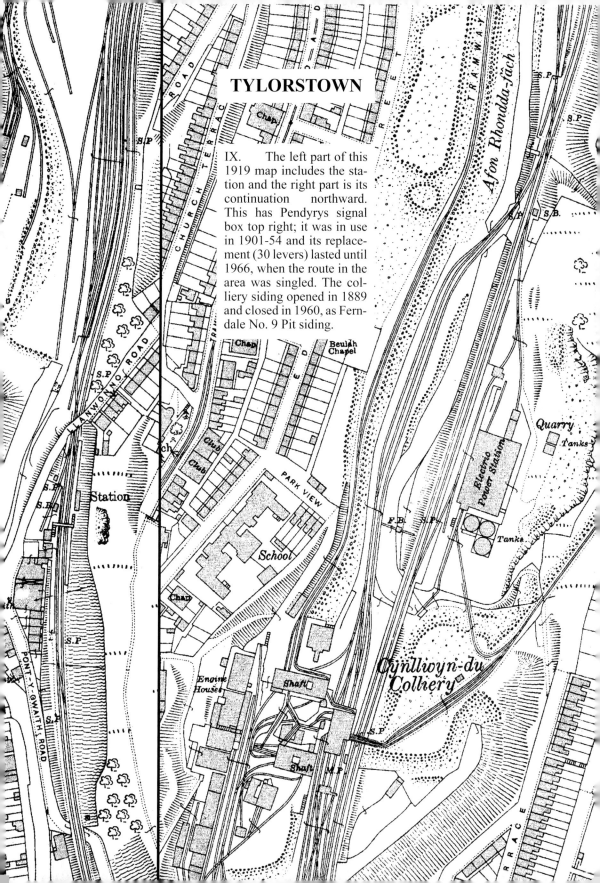

TYLORSTOWN

IX. The left part of this 1919 map includes the station and the right part is its continuation northward. This has Pendyrys signal box top right; it was in use in 1901-54 and its replacement (30 levers) lasted until 1966, when the route in the area was singled. The colliery siding opened in 1889 and closed in 1960, as Ferndale No. 9 Pit siding.

Afon Rhondda-fach

TRAMWAY

S.P.

S.P.

S.P.

S.B.

Chap.

CHURCH TERRACE

ROAD

STREET

Quarry

Tanks

Electric Power Station

Chap

Beulah Chapel

ANWONWG ROAD

S.P.

Club

Club

PARK VIEW

F.B.

S.P.

Tanks

Station

S.P.

S.B.

School

Chap

Tanks

PONT-Y-GWAITH ROAD

S.P.

S.P.

Engine House

Shaft

Cynllwyn-du Colliery

S.P.

Shaft M.P.

TERRACE

31.　　The station opened on 24th May 1882 and this northward view from around 1910 has advertisements for VIM, an abrasive cleaning material much needed locally in the era before detergents. Staff numbered 15 in 1923 and 10 in 1937. (Lens of Sutton coll.)

32.　　The short siding was in use from about 1907 to 1963 and the 22-lever signal box served until 31st August 1966. The background gives an impression of the depth of the valley. (P.J.Garland/R.S.Carpenter coll.)

33.　　Coal from Maerdy passes the site of the colliery on 25th March 1976, hauled by no. 37275. The river will soon erode the remainder of the trackbed. (T.Heavyside)

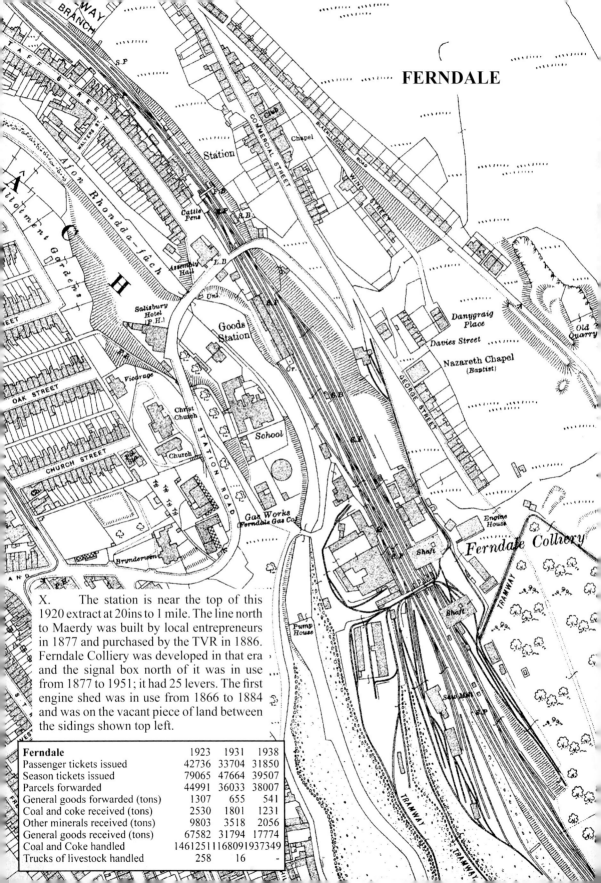

FERNDALE

X.   The station is near the top of this 1920 extract at 20ins to 1 mile. The line north to Maerdy was built by local entrepreneurs in 1877 and purchased by the TVR in 1886. Ferndale Colliery was developed in that era and the signal box north of it was in use from 1877 to 1951; it had 25 levers. The first engine shed was in use from 1866 to 1884 and was on the vacant piece of land between the sidings shown top left.

Ferndale	1923	1931	1938
Passenger tickets issued	42736	33704	31850
Season tickets issued	79065	47664	39507
Parcels forwarded	44991	36033	38007
General goods forwarded (tons)	1307	655	541
Coal and coke received (tons)	2530	1801	1231
Other minerals received (tons)	9803	3518	2056
General goods received (tons)	67582	31794	17774
Coal and Coke handled	146125	116809	193 7349
Trucks of livestock handled	258	16	-

34.   Miners were conveyed here from 1868 to March 1875. Public traffic began on 5th June 1876. The colliery in the background of this southward panorama emphasises the proximity of the dwellings. The small signal box on the left was replaced by the one in the next picture in about 1920. (Lens of Sutton coll.)

35.   Looking north in 1922, we have the cattle dock on the left and the 52-lever Ferndale Upper box on the right. It was renamed Station box in 1952 and was closed on 14th June 1964. (D.K.Jones coll.)

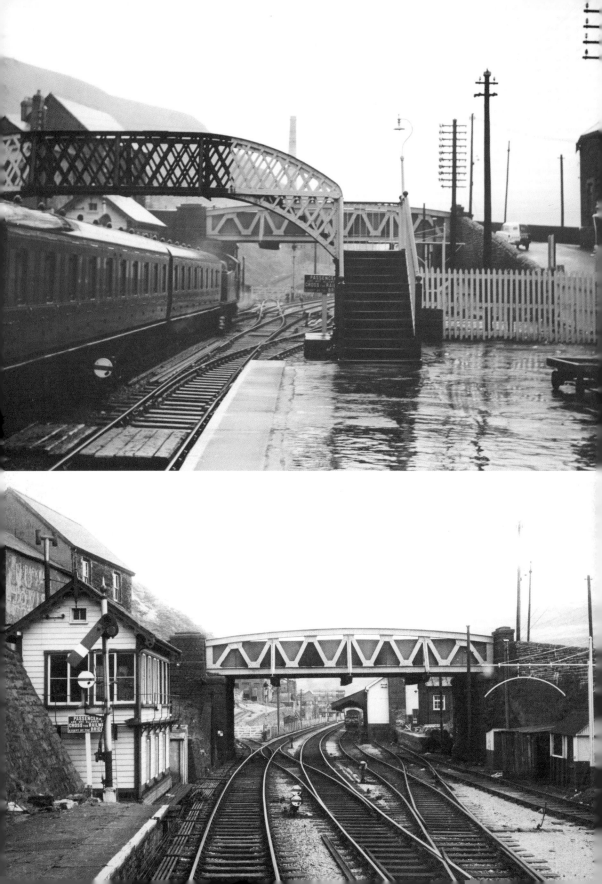

← 36. The 2.25pm to Cardiff leaves in heavy rain on 7th April 1962, behind 2-6-2T no. 5632. The short siding behind the steps had gone by 1936. In 1923, 78 men had been needed, but only 45 by 1937. (M.A.N.Johnston)

← 37. An uncluttered view in the same direction on 17th August 1963 features the long and narrow goods shed and the gate over the private siding to the colliery. (P.J.Garland/R.S.Carpenter coll.)

38. We look at the other end of the goods shed on the same day and find the jib of the 5-ton crane protruding above it. The goods yard closed on 7th October 1963. Eleven private sidings had been listed in 1938. (P.J.Garland/R.S.Carpenter coll.)

JUN.9.15

T. V. R.
MAERDY
TO
FERNDALE
Parly. Third Class 2d.
This ticket is issued subject to the Company's Bye-Laws & conditions stated on Time Bills.

3192

2 JAN 25

Taff Vale Railway
Parly Third Class 1/8
MAERDY
TO
BLAENGWYNFY (R&SB)
Via TREHERBERT
SEE NOTE ON BACK

REVISED FARE 27/7/3

1454

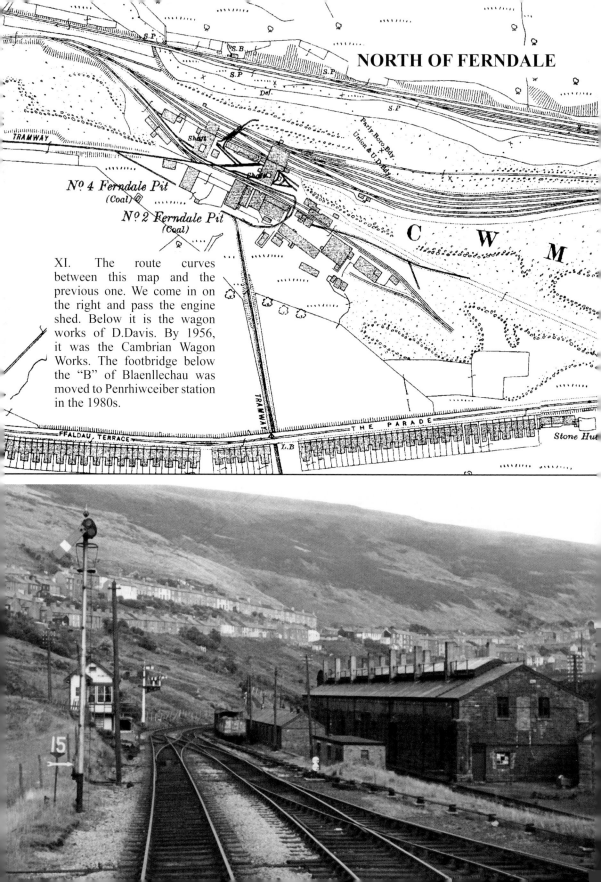

TRAMWAY

No 4 Ferndale Pit
(Coal)

No 2 Ferndale Pit
(Coal)

Shaft

Shaft

Party Boro Bdy
Union & U D Bdy

S.P

S.B

S.P

S.P

Def.

C W M

XI. The route curves between this map and the previous one. We come in on the right and pass the engine shed. Below it is the wagon works of D.Davis. By 1956, it was the Cambrian Wagon Works. The footbridge below the "B" of Blaenllechau was moved to Penrhiwceiber station in the 1980s.

TRAMWAY

FFALDAU TERRACE

L.B

THE PARADE

Stone Hut

15

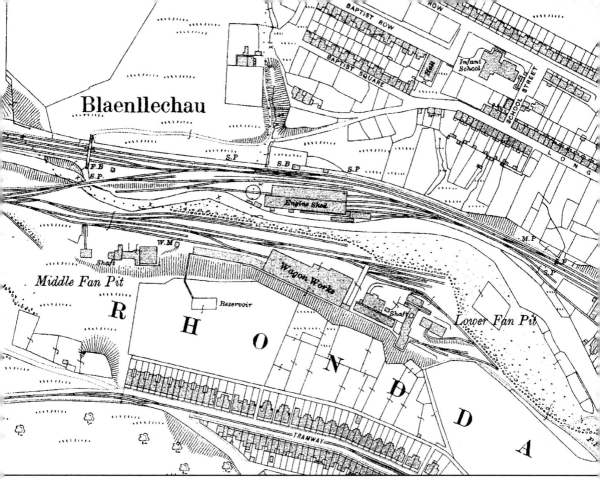

Blaenllechau

Middle Fan Pit

R H O N D D A

39. Ferndale engine shed was completed by the TVR in 1884 and its west end is seen in August 1963, along with Maerdy Branch Junction box, which was in use from 1889. It had 35 levers and functioned until 19th December 1966. (P.J.Garland/R.S.Carpenter coll.)

40. The engine shed was reduced from four roads to two in 1931 and the turntable was removed in 1938. The shed is seen in 1958 and was closed in September 1964. It was coded 88 by the GWR and sub to 88F by BR. It had 16 0-6-2Ts at the end of 1947. (D.K.Jones coll.)

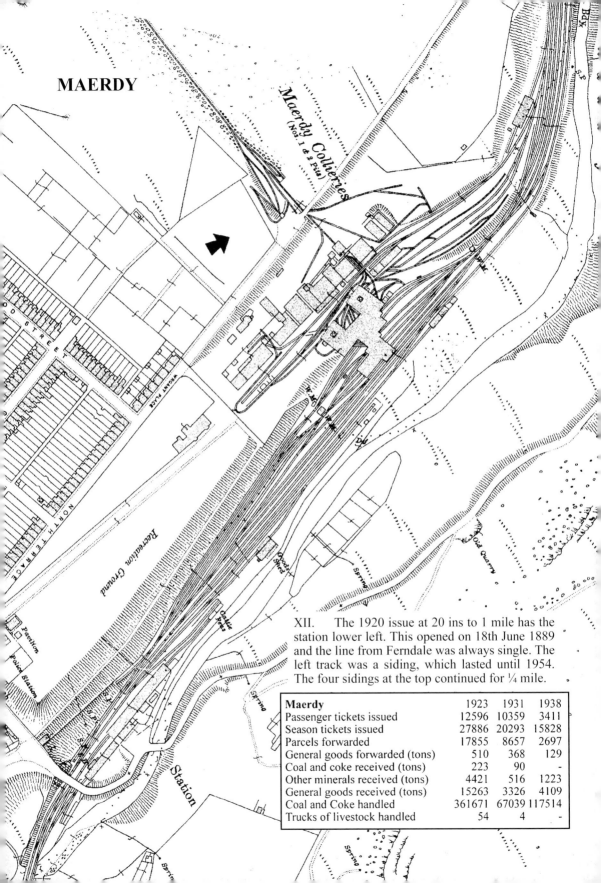

MAERDY

Maerdy Collieries (Nos. 1 & 2 Pits)

Recreation Ground

Goods Shed

Cattle Pens

Station

XII.   The 1920 issue at 20 ins to 1 mile has the station lower left. This opened on 18th June 1889 and the line from Ferndale was always single. The left track was a siding, which lasted until 1954. The four sidings at the top continued for ¼ mile.

Maerdy	1923	1931	1938
Passenger tickets issued	12596	10359	3411
Season tickets issued	27886	20293	15828
Parcels forwarded	17855	8657	2697
General goods forwarded (tons)	510	368	129
Coal and coke received (tons)	223	90	-
Other minerals received (tons)	4421	516	1223
General goods received (tons)	15263	3326	4109
Coal and Coke handled	361671	67039	117514
Trucks of livestock handled	54	4	

41.   A fine southward panorama includes three chapels together with crowds walking towards the station for the opening ceremony. The long building in this and the next view was the carriage shed. At over 900 ft above sea level, trains would be snow covered and frozen frequently without such protection. Staff dropped from 19 in 1923 to 10 in 1935. (Lens of Sutton coll.)

42.   The storage sidings can be seen above the signal box, which had a 65-lever frame. No. 5574 is waiting to leave with the 12.25pm to Porth on 6th November 1957. Beyond the left signal is the small goods yard, which closed on 1st March 1956. (H.Ballantyne)

43.   A Porth service was recorded on 21st August 1963. Other pictures show that we are above the tree line, but here a few specimens have had the benefit of shelter within the cutting. The box closed on 14th June 1964. (P.J.Garland/R.S.Carpenter coll.)

44.   The crosses on the wagons indicate that they must not leave the site. This was substantially redeveloped in 1956 and its spelling was altered to Mardy. A Peckett 0-6-0ST is shunting on 7th October 1971; pit closure came on 21st October 1990. (T.Heavyside)

DINAS RHONDDA

45.   We return to the main route and after leaving Porth it passes the site of Tynewydd Colliery (closed 1906), Dinas Colliery (closed 1928), Upper Cymmer Colliery (closed 1935) and Pandy station

Dinas	1923	1931	1938
Passenger tickets issued	41425	36527	31591
Season tickets issued	371	489	437
Parcels forwarded	4757	4603	2092

(closed 1886). Dinas station was then built to the west of it. The suffix "Rhondda" was used from 1st November 1927 to 12th May 1980 and again from 28th May 2000. (Lens of Sutton coll.)

46.   Approaching the station on 12th May 1956 is 0-6-0PT no. 8460 with empty wagons for loading further up the valley. The siding to Naval Colliery ran between the station and the river until 22nd November 1965. Naval Colliery Junction box is on the right and closed on 22nd November 1965. It had 40 levers. Twelve men were needed in 1923 and ten in the 1930s. (J&J coll.)

47.   The station was closed as a wartime economy measure from 2nd April 1917 to 1st July 1919. It is seen in 1958; the roadbridge on the left spans the line to Naval Colliery. It did not belong to the Navy, but supplied it in the early years of the century. (Stations UK)

48.   The centre track was lost in November 1964 and the one nearest to us was taken out of use on 31st March 1981. We see the 13.00 Barry Island to Treherbert on the former down line on 29th June of that year. In the distance is Porth's distant signal. (T.Heavyside)

TONYPANDY

49.   The station opened on 9th March 1908 as Trealaw and became Tonypandy & Trealaw on 1st September 1909, losing its suffix on 7th May 1973. There was a staff of 45 in 1929 and 30 in 1938. (Lens of Sutton coll.)

50.   A poorly reproduced postcard gives a record of the proximity of Naval Colliery and the position of the footbridge over its connecting line. Both appear in the next view, rather dramatically.
(Lens of Sutton coll.)

Tonypandy	1923	1931	1938
Passenger tickets issued	162800	158172	112262
Season tickets issued	1149	2039	1425
Parcels forwarded	76266	58154	52391
General goods forwarded (tons)	1690	1363	1179
Coal and coke received (tons)	423	493	2490
Other minerals received (tons)	6015	3120	2683
General goods received (tons)	24636	54294	36528
Coal and Coke handled	264467	970672	851935
Trucks of livestock handled	130	428	244

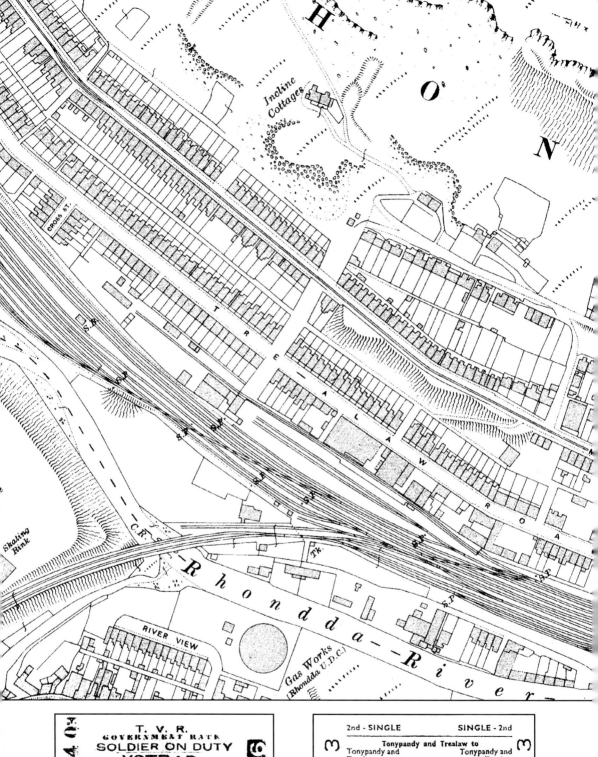

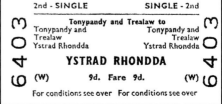

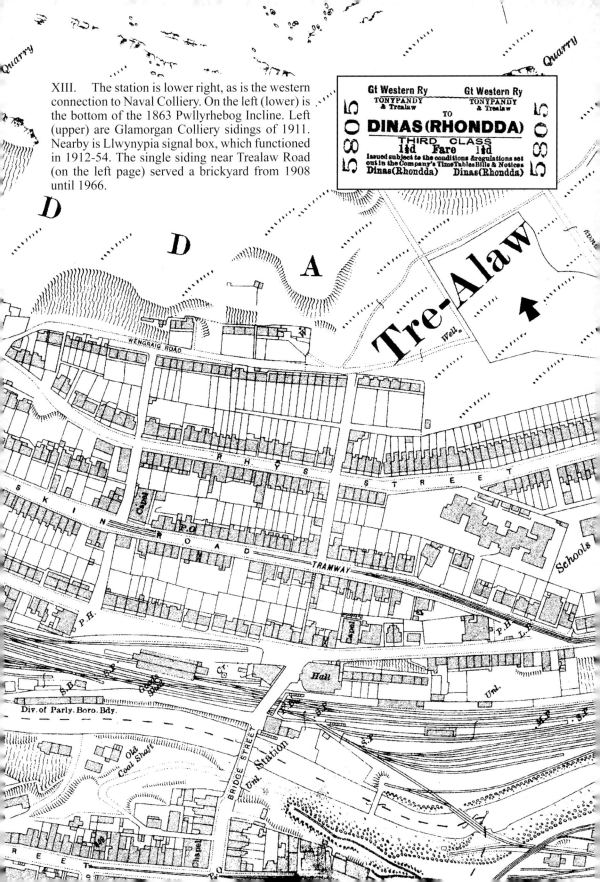

XIII. The station is lower right, as is the western connection to Naval Colliery. On the left (lower) is the bottom of the 1863 Pwllyrhebog Incline. Left (upper) are Glamorgan Colliery sidings of 1911. Nearby is Llwynypia signal box, which functioned in 1912-54. The single siding near Trealaw Road (on the left page) served a brickyard from 1908 until 1966.

Gt Western Ry
TONYPANDY
& Trealaw
TO
DINAS (RHONDDA)
THIRD CLASS
Fare 1½d
Issued subject to the conditions & regulations set out in the Company's Time Tables Bills & Notices
Dinas (Rhondda)

Gt Western Ry
TONYPANDY
& Trealaw
TO
DINAS (RHONDDA)
1½d
Dinas (Rhondda)

5805 5805

D

D A

Tre-Alaw

Well.

Quarry

Quarry

WENGRAIG ROAD

RHYS STREET

Chapel

P.O.

SKIN ROAD

TRAMWAY

Schools

P.H.

Chapel

P.H.

S.B.

Div. of Parly. Boro. Bdy.

Goods Shed

Hall

Unl.

Old Coal Shaft

BRIDGE STREET

Unl. Station

REE T

Chapel

51.　　A 1951 photograph shows some protection from the rain and that down passengers also had a screen against the west wind. The siding to Naval Colliery closed in October 1958. (H.C.Casserley)

52.　　Passing Pwllyrhebog signal box and the 6-ton crane on 12th May 1956 is 0-6-0PT no. 8419. The goods yard closed on 31st January 1966. (J&J coll.)

53.   The west end of the station was photographed on 14th April 1962. It was unstaffed from 2nd February 1970. The 48-lever signal box closed on 22nd August 1966. (B.W.L.Brooksbank)

Table 142	SWANSEA, NEATH, ABERAVON, and TREHERBERT																			June 1950
Miles		**Week Days only**																		
		a.m	a.m	a.m	a.m	a.m	a.m	a.m	a.m	p.m	p.m	p.m	p.m		p.m	p.m	p.m	p.m	p.m	p.m
		S	E	X			V		S							X				U
	Treherbert........ dep	7 20		7 50			9 38	1119	1155			1 45	2 30			5 44		7 31			1034	
½	Blaenrhondda........	7 24		7 54			9 42	1123	1159			1 50	2 34			5 48		7 35			1038	
3½	Blaengwynfi........	7 34		8 4			9 52	1133	12 9			2 0	2 44	5 0		5 58		7 45			1048	
6	Cymmer Afan........	7 40		8 10			9 59	1139	1215			2 6	2 58	5 6		6 6		7 52			1054	
7¼	Duffryn Rhondda Halt	7 44		8 14			10 3		1219			3	3 5	5 10		6 10		7 56			1059	
8½	Cynonville Halt........	7 49		8 19			10 7		1224			3	7	5 14		6 14		8 0			11 4	
10½	Pontrhydyfen........	7 54		8 24			1013	1151	1229			3 12	6 19			6 20		8 5			11 9	
12	Cwmavon........	8 2		8 31			1020	12 2	1236			3 19	5 26			6 27		8 12			1116	
13½	Aberavon (Town) A { arr	8 9		8 38			1027	12 9	1243			3 27	5 33			6 34		8 20			1123	
	dep	8 12		8 41			1029	1212	1245			3 28				6 39		8 21			1125	
14½	Aberavon (Seaside)	8 16		8 45			1033		1249			3 32				6 42		8 25				
16½	Bagla n Sands Halt......																				
17½	Briton Ferry........	8 24		8 53			1041	1224	1257			3 41				6 50		8 36				
19	Neath (General)........	8 29	8 45	8 58	9	7 9 21	1054		1 2	1 12	1 39	3 47			6 55	7 38	4 18	54	9 1	1140	
21	Skewen........					9 27	11 0				1 45	3 53				7 8		9 7			
24	Llansamlet North					9 33	11 6				1 51	3 59				7 12		9 13			
26	Landore					9 39	1112				1 57	4 5				7 17		9 19			
27½	Swansea (High St.) ..arr		9 1		9 20	9 44	1117			1 29	2 2	4 10				7 21		9 8	9 24		

A About ¼ mile from Port Talbot (General) Station
E Except Saturdays
S Saturdays only
U Thursdays and Saturdays; also daily during August

V Saturdays only. Runs 23rd July to 2nd September inclusive. Through Train Cardiff (Queen St.) to Aberystwyth arr. 3 50 p.m. (Tables 125, 104, and 146)
X Third class only, limited accommodation

Z Saturdays only. Runs 29th July to 2nd September inclusive. Through Train Aberystwyth to Cardiff (Queen Street) arr. 8 45 p.m. (Tables 146, 104, and 125)
A Third Class only

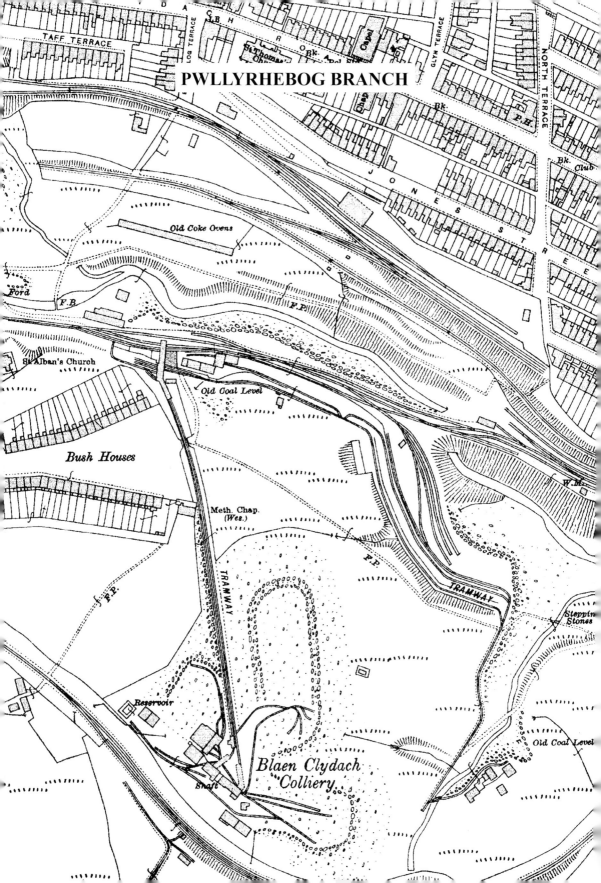

PWLLYRHEBOG BRANCH

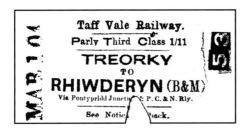

XIV.   The top of the ¾ mile long incline from Tonypandy is in the centre of the right page of this 1920 map. Blaen Clydach goods shed is in the centre of the left one and two reversals were needed to reach it. The 1899 line to Clydach Vale Colliery continues top left. It closed in 1951. Curving across the bottom is part of the Ely & Clydach Valleys Railway of 1878. Closure came in 1967. Its route is shown on map II.

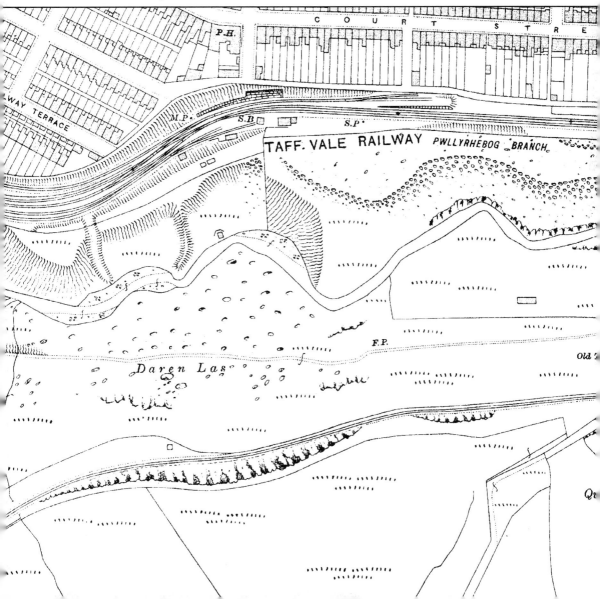

54.   We have four photographs from 4th May 1951 to illustrate the incline and we start at the bottom, just above the gasworks on map XIII. No. 195 was one of three 0-6-0Ts built in 1884 by Kitsons with special tapered boilers for use on the incline. They had large wheels to give clearance above the cable. (P.J.Garland/R.S.Carpenter coll.)

55.   We look towards the top of the incline and find the signal box and winding house, plus the cables disappearing underground to the drums. These were steam powered and they also allowed trains to be balanced. A locomotive was required on each track for additional power and braking the short trains of usually 8 or 9 wagons. Parts of the gradient were 1 in 13. (H.C.Casserley)

56.   This view from the summit was taken from the curve in the background of the previous picture. The winding drums were linked by gears and the winding engine worked at only 25psi. (H.C.Casserley)

57.   Two locomotives were kept in this shed at the top of the incline, while the third was sent to Treherbert for servicing. The shed closed in July 1951 and the incline followed on 2nd April 1955, officially. The shed does not show on the map, as it was built in 1919, the year of the survey. The shed code was sub to 88F in BR days. (H.C.Casserley)

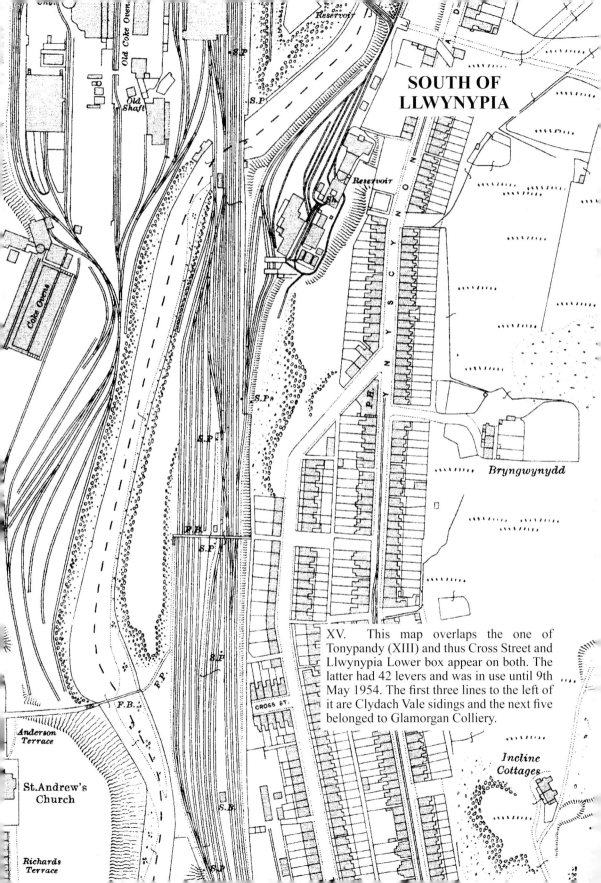

SOUTH OF LLWYNYPIA

Reservoir

Reservoir

Old Coke Oven

Old Shaft

Coke Ovens

Coke Ovens

Bryngwynydd

XV. This map overlaps the one of Tonypandy (XIII) and thus Cross Street and Llwynypia Lower box appear on both. The latter had 42 levers and was in use until 9th May 1954. The first three lines to the left of it are Clydach Vale sidings and the next five belonged to Glamorgan Colliery.

CROSS ST.

Incline Cottages

Anderson Terrace

St. Andrew's Church

Richards Terrace

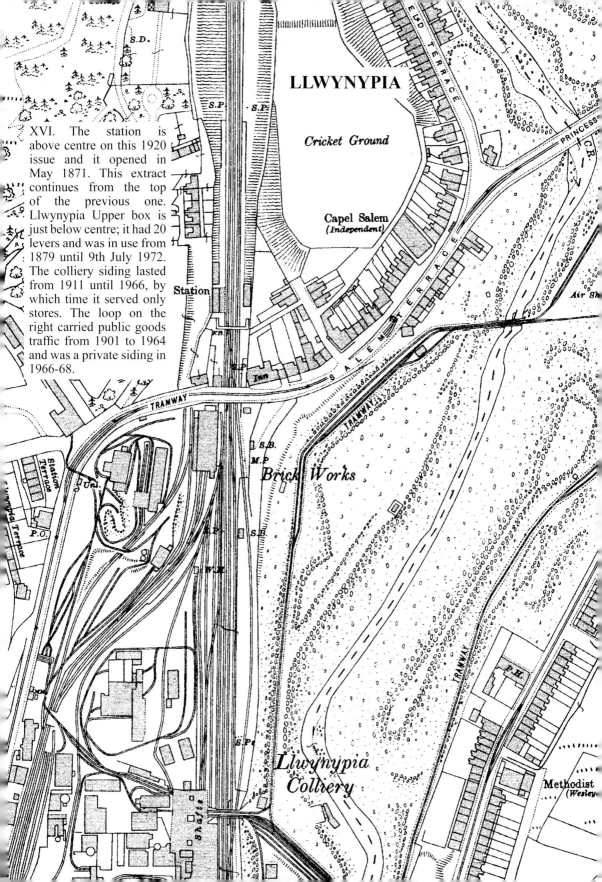

LLWYNYPIA

Cricket Ground

Capel Salem
(Independent)

XVI. The station is above centre on this 1920 issue and it opened in May 1871. This extract continues from the top of the previous one. Llwynypia Upper box is just below centre; it had 20 levers and was in use from 1879 until 9th July 1972. The colliery siding lasted from 1911 until 1966, by which time it served only stores. The loop on the right carried public goods traffic from 1901 to 1964 and was a private siding in 1966-68.

Station

Brick Works

Llwynypia
Colliery

Methodist
(Wesley

S.D.

S.P.   S.P.

SALEM TERRACE

TRAMWAY

Station Terrace

P.O.

Inn

S.B.

M.P.

S.B.

TRAMWAY

Shafts

S.P.

PRINCESS

Air Sh

58. Looking north, there are no signs of industry; they are all behind us. The suffix "& Tonypandy" was used until 9th March 1908. There had been 18 men in 1923 and 10 in 1935. (J.Langford coll.)

59. The centre track was in use from 1875 until 1964 and the nearest one ceased to be used in March 1981. No. 5693 is working the 3.30pm Treherbert to Barry Island on 12th May 1956. (J&J coll.)

60.   Staffing ceased on 1st December 1969 and this is the scene on 12th August 1984. Standard platform shelters arrived subsequently. (D.K.Jones)

NORTH OF LLWYNYPIA

XVII.   One mile north of Llwynypia was the gasworks siding, which was in use from 1886 until 1955. The sidings branching at the top ran to Bodringallt Colliery and Cymric Rhondda Colliery. The connection was in traffic between 1894 and 1955.

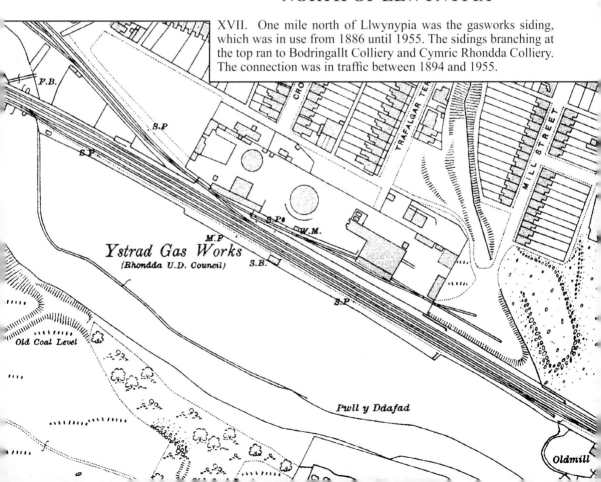

YSTRAD RHONDDA

61.   This name was applied initially to a station one mile north, but that has been Ton Pentre since 28th September 1986, when this new station opened, together with a passing loop. This southward view is from the opening day. (D.K.Jones coll.)

62.   The 12.50 Penarth to Treherbert departs north on 6th November 1986. The new loop enabled a 30-minute interval service to be operated on the branch. (T.Heavyside)

63.   This northward view from 13th February 2009 shows the driver of the 09.06 from Cardiff Central observing single line working procedures being undertaken in the unmarked hut. (V.Mitchell)

64.   In the hut, communication is necessary with the panel at Radyr before the electrical system can release the token for the next section. It will be checked by the driver. (V.Mitchell)

Taff Vale Railway.
Parly Third Class 1/11½
YSTRAD
TO
BASSALEG (B&M)
Via Pontypridd & P. C. & N. Ry.
SEE NOTICE ON B'CK.

Ystrad	1923	1931	1938
Passenger tickets issued	163784	144129	97969
Season tickets issued	967	1355	911
Parcels forwarded	70984	59765	46146
General goods forwarded (tons)	1731		
Coal and coke received (tons)	7306		
Other minerals received (tons)	10312	with Treorchy	
General goods received (tons)	44983		
Coal and Coke handled	752666		
Trucks of livestock handled	473		

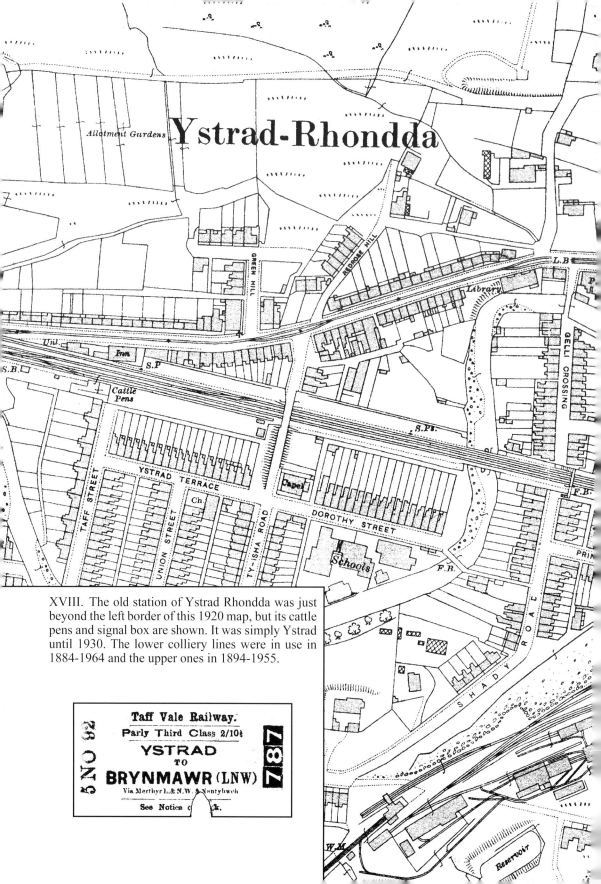

Allotment Gardens **Ystrad-Rhondda**

XVIII. The old station of Ystrad Rhondda was just beyond the left border of this 1920 map, but its cattle pens and signal box are shown. It was simply Ystrad until 1930. The lower colliery lines were in use in 1884-1964 and the upper ones in 1894-1955.

Taff Vale Railway.
Parly Third Class 2/10½
YSTRAD
TO
BRYNMAWR (LNW)
Via Merthyr L.& N.W. & Nantybwch
See Notice on back.

5 NO 83

787

Bodringallt Colliery

Sh.

Shaft

BODRINGALLT TERRACE

Chapel Nebo
url.Gd.

P.H.

ARTHUR

Bethel Chapel
(Calv.Meth.)

Un. W I L L I A M

P.H.

F.B.

M

S T R E E T

ROAD

P.O.

S.P.

S.P.

S.P.

W.M.

W.M.

W.M.

S.

Old Coke Ovens

Gelli Collieries

Shaft

r Shaft

Gelli Terrace

Reservoir

TON PENTRE

65.   Ystrad Rhondda's down platform was well sheltered and a massive screen was provided in front of the door to the well ventilated facilities for gentlemen. The goods yard closed on 3rd August 1964. A staff of 47 was needed in 1923 and 26 in 1934.
(Lens of Sutton coll.)

66.   Beyond the brake van in this photograph from October 1954 is Ystrad Rhondda signal box. This was the name of the station also from 1930 to 1986. The box had 35 levers and closed on 9th January 1966.
(Lens of Sutton coll.)

67.   The   1970s standard shelter had the barge boards turquoise and the brickwork painted red.   There   were   no patrons for the 09.06 from Cardiff Central on 13th February 2009, when the mountains had received a picturesque dusting of snow. (V.Mitchell)

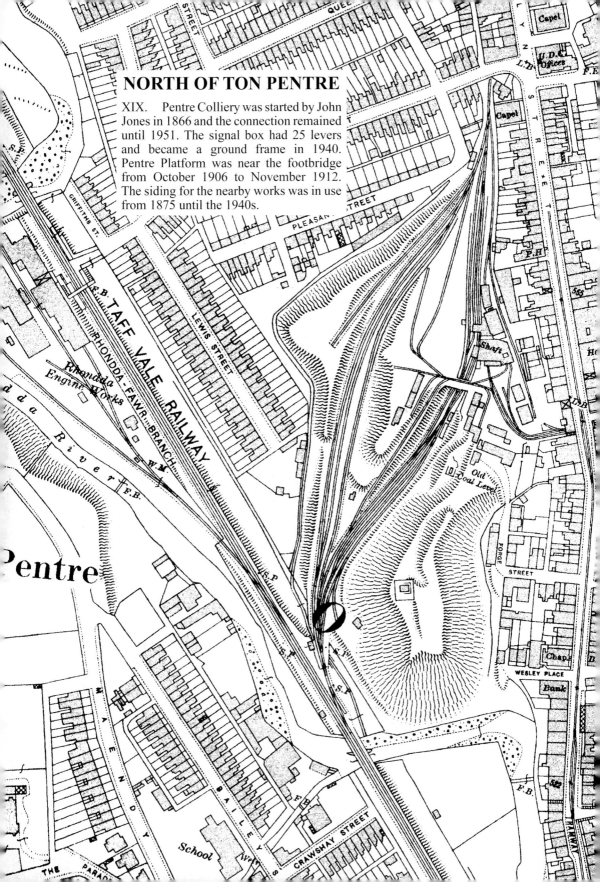

NORTH OF TON PENTRE

XIX.   Pentre Colliery was started by John Jones in 1866 and the connection remained until 1951. The signal box had 25 levers and became a ground frame in 1940. Pentre Platform was near the footbridge from October 1906 to November 1912. The siding for the nearby works was in use from 1875 until the 1940s.

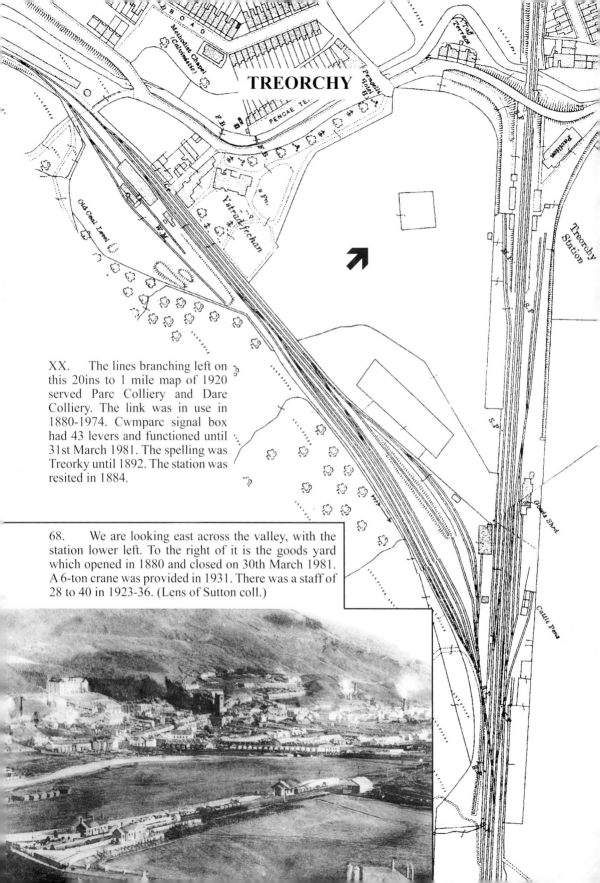

TREORCHY

XX.   The lines branching left on this 20ins to 1 mile map of 1920 served Parc Colliery and Dare Colliery. The link was in use in 1880-1974. Cwmparc signal box had 43 levers and functioned until 31st March 1981. The spelling was Treorky until 1892. The station was resited in 1884.

68.   We are looking east across the valley, with the station lower left. To the right of it is the goods yard which opened in 1880 and closed on 30th March 1981. A 6-ton crane was provided in 1931. There was a staff of 28 to 40 in 1923-36. (Lens of Sutton coll.)

69.   A down freight train hauled by a TVR 0-6-0 rumbles through, before canopies were provided. It was later unusual to see a tender engine in a Welsh valley and there are few views of a somersault signal off, either. (Lens of Sutton coll.)

70.   A down DMU was recorded on 12th January 1960, with the goods shed in the distance on the left of the tracks. The first station was ½ mile up the valley and was in use from 27th September 1869 until 3rd March 1884. (D.K.Jones coll.)

Treorchy	1923	1931	1938
Passenger tickets issued	108556	98457	77873
Season tickets issued	1017	1126	656
Parcels forwarded	50568	45032	41428
General goods forwarded (tons)	3313	2316	4984
Coal and coke received (tons)	2319	820	5373
Other minerals received (tons)	7032	1769	6314
General goods received (tons)	39293	22708	58161
Coal and Coke handled	922583	609331	841849
Trucks of livestock handled	250	116	866

YNYSWEN

71.   This stop opened on 29th September 1986, but only in factory hours until 10th May 1987. The platform is on the east side of the line. (D.K.Jones coll.)

72.   A photograph from February 2009 shows a well wooded location, the trees stretching for more than a mile westwards. Most furnishings had changed since the previous picture. (V.Mitchell)

SOUTH OF TREHERBERT

XXI.   Curving away from the straight TVR route is the line to Abergorchwy Colliery, which had four different spellings. The siding was in use between about 1875 and 1950. The first station for Treorchy had been near the platforms and footbridge shown here. They are those of Tylacoch Halt, which was open from October 1906 to November 1912. The colliery south thereof had a siding in 1855-95. Further north along the main line was a branch to Ynysfeio Colliery which was in use from 1857 to 1951. The signal box of that name had 50 levers and closed in 1958.

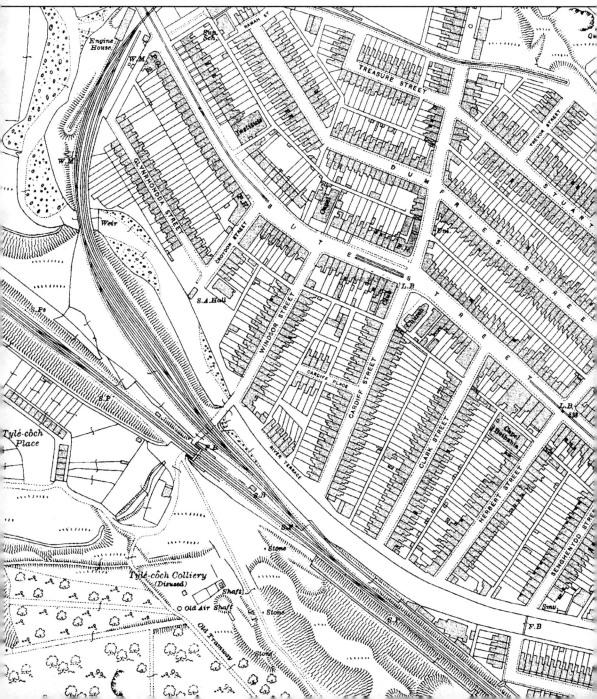

TREHERBERT

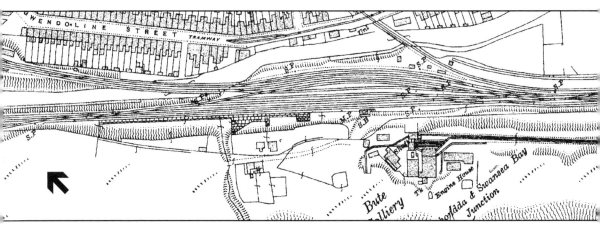

XXII.   On the right page of this 1920 map at 20ins to 1 mile is the station, goods shed and Lady Margaret Colliery. The engine shed lasted until 1931. The TVR continues straight across the left page, destined for Fernhill Colliery. The route closed on 5th December 1966. The R&SBR diverges from it on the left, with its engine shed on the left border. It closed in 1922. At the top is the line to Rhondda Merthyr Colliery, which had closed in about 1906. Known as Rhondda & Swansea Bay Junction, the 60-lever signal box closed on 12th April 1964.

73.   A northward panorama from an early postcard has Lady Margaret Colliery on the left, with the curved roof of the engine shed beyond it (right). The two long parallel sheds were for carriages and were demolished in 1913. The staff numbered 114 in 1923 and 88 in 1937.
(Lens of Sutton coll.)

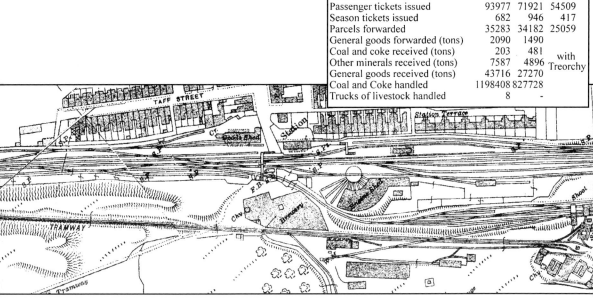

Treherbert	1923	1931	1938
Passenger tickets issued	93977	71921	54509
Season tickets issued	682	946	417
Parcels forwarded	35283	34182	25059
General goods forwarded (tons)	2090	1490	
Coal and coke received (tons)	203	481	
Other minerals received (tons)	7587	4896	with Treorchy
General goods received (tons)	43716	27270	
Coal and Coke handled	1198408	827728	
Trucks of livestock handled	8	-	

74.   Looking east, part of the station is on the right and the goods shed is centre. One wagon door is down, revealing just WC! Its contents would have been for domestic use - local coal had a high combustion temperature, too great for open hearths. The yard had a 3-ton crane and closed on 5th August 1963. (Lens of Sutton coll.)

75.   The new engine shed was built near the top right corner of the map and is seen in 1931, together with the standard GWR coal stage with the water tank acting as the roof. There were 37 locos here in 1926. (GWR)

76. A flat-topped tip dominated the northward view on 27th June 1938. The tall coach on the right is ex-Barry Railway. (H.C.Casserley)

77. The Lady Margaret Colliery siding was in use from 1879 until 1950 and the headgear could still be seen when this photograph was taken on 27th August 1959. The 9.30am from Barry Island is on the left and the 11.25 to Swansea is on the right. In the distance is South Box (49 levers); it served from 1931 to 27th September 1965. (S.P.Derek)

78. The finger boards could be slid in place by the staff. This 1960 view includes the new shelter for men undertaking diesel fuelling and little evidence of the colliery. (D.K.Jones coll.)

79.   The 1931 engine shed was fitted with continuous smoke hoods and was similar to the one at Radyr. Its allocation in December 1947 was one 2-6-2T, twenty-three 0-6-2Ts, one 0-6-0PT and three 0-6-0Ts. Nearest on 1st April 1961 is 0-6-2T no. 5693. The shed closed in March 1965. (P.J.Kelley)

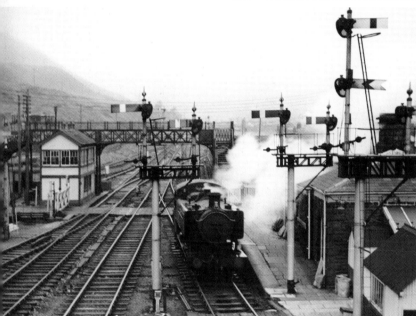

80.   North box is featured on 7th April 1962 as 0-6-0PT no. 8439 runs round its train. The short platform and the small building are of note. The latter was in use by train crews in 2009, having only recently retired as a ticket office. The box had 52 levers when it closed on 27th November 1972, when the line was singled to Cwmparc. (M.A.N.Johnston)

81.   An arrival was recorded on 6th November 1986, by which time fuelling was undertaken in Cardiff. Four sidings remained in 2010 for berthing, plus a loop, behind the camera. (T.Heavyside)

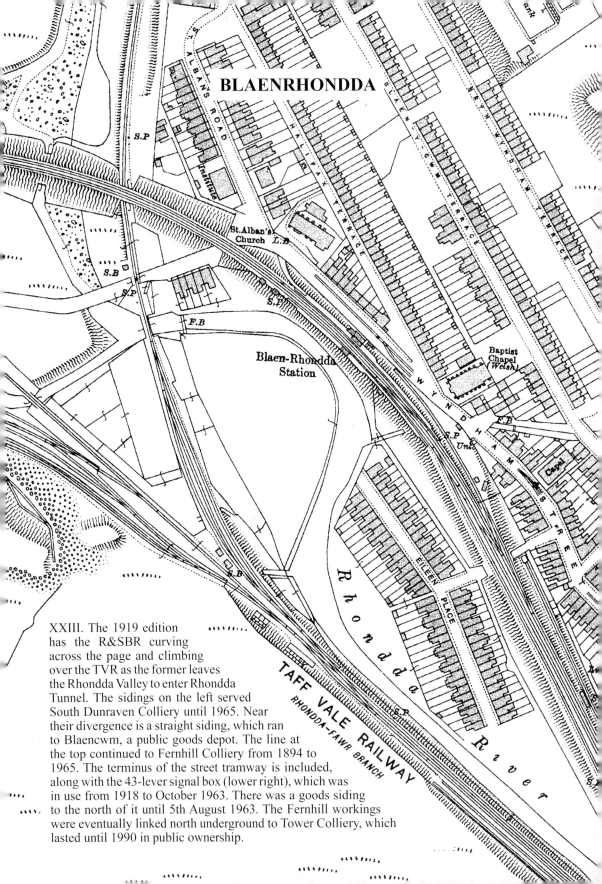

BLAENRHONDDA

St.Alban's Church *L.B*

Blaen-Rhondda Station

Baptist Chapel (Welsh)

Chapel

Rhondda River

XXIII. The 1919 edition has the R&SBR curving across the page and climbing over the TVR as the former leaves the Rhondda Valley to enter Rhondda Tunnel. The sidings on the left served South Dunraven Colliery until 1965. Near their divergence is a straight siding, which ran to Blaencwm, a public goods depot. The line at the top continued to Fernhill Colliery from 1894 to 1965. The terminus of the street tramway is included, along with the 43-lever signal box (lower right), which was in use from 1918 to October 1963. There was a goods siding to the north of it until 5th August 1963. The Fernhill workings were eventually linked north underground to Tower Colliery, which lasted until 1990 in public ownership.

TAFF VALE RAILWAY

RHONDDA-FAWR BRANCH

82. The bleak landscape was recorded on a postcard in about 1910. The ornate lamps were some compensation. There were 14 men employed here in 1923 and 11 in 1931.
(Lens of Sutton coll.)

83. This is the 10.40am R&SB Junction to Briton Ferry freight working on 12th January 1960. It is hauled by 0-6-2T no. 6605.
(J&J coll.)

84. Poor weather on 7th April 1962 dulls this record of 0-6-2T no. 5687 running light engine. It was taken from a Neath to Treherbert train, hauled by 0-6-0PT no. 8439. Staffing ceased on 20th September 1965.
(M.A.N.Johnston)

WEST OF BLAENRHONDDA

XXIV. The 1946 map is scaled at 2 miles to 1ins and has Treherbert top right, the tunnel starting above its T. Cymmer is the junction of four lines, with services being operated to Port Talbot until 1962 and between Treherbert and Bridgend (lower right) until 1968. Glyncorrwg had a passenger service between 1918 and 1930, but miners trains for longer.

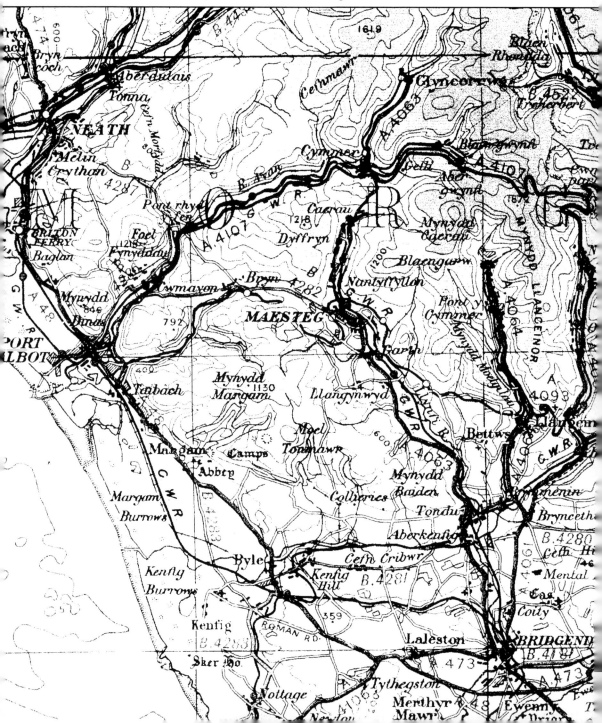

85. We are approaching Rhondda Tunnel on 10th November 1967 and have the sidings of Glen Rhondda Colliery on the left. They were in use in 1907-1967. On the right is Blaen y Cwm box, which had 15 levers and closed with the line in 1968. The bridge carried a colliery tramway. (M.Dart)

86. The tunnel length was 3443yds and the structure was always a great cause of concern. These alarming leaks were photographed on 2nd March 1922. Locomotive crews had to position themselves carefully in their cabs. It was such extreme conditions that demanded the sudden closure on 26th February 1968. (GWR)

BLAENGWYNFI

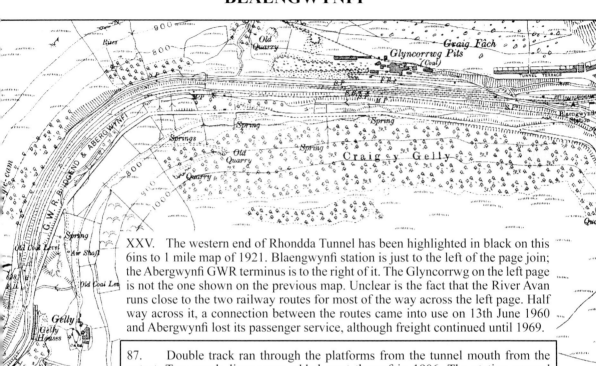

XXV.   The western end of Rhondda Tunnel has been highlighted in black on this 6ins to 1 mile map of 1921. Blaengwynfi station is just to the left of the page join; the Abergwynfi GWR terminus is to the right of it. The Glyncorrwg on the left page is not the one shown on the previous map. Unclear is the fact that the River Avan runs close to the two railway routes for most of the way across the left page. Half way across it, a connection between the routes came into use on 13th June 1960 and Abergwynfi lost its passenger service, although freight continued until 1969.

87.   Double track ran through the platforms from the tunnel mouth from the outset. Two goods lines were added west thereof in 1906. The station opened exactly one month before Blaenrhondda and had 13 men in 1923, but only 8 in 1933. (P.J.Garland/R.S.Carpenter coll.)

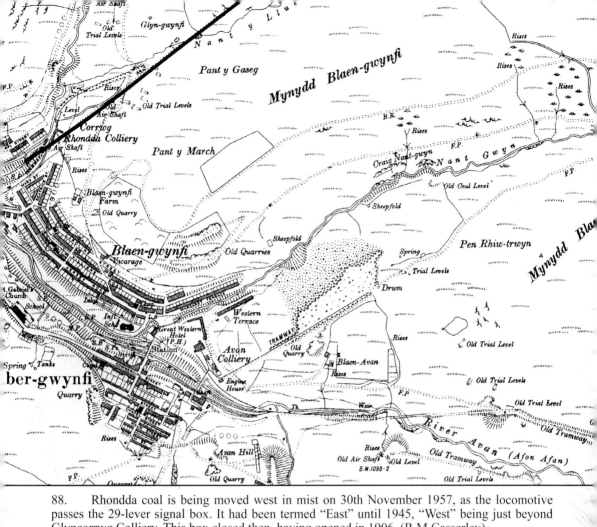

88.   Rhondda coal is being moved west in mist on 30th November 1957, as the locomotive passes the 29-lever signal box. It had been termed "East" until 1945, "West" being just beyond Glyncorrwg Colliery. This box closed then, having opened in 1906. (R.M.Casserley)

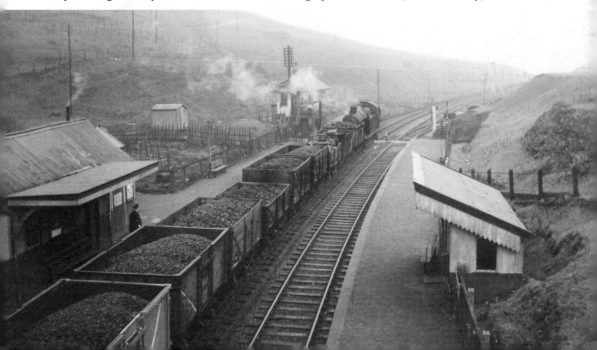

89.   The contorted landscape is evident as a DMU emerges from Rhondda Tunnel, working the 2.30pm Treherbert to Swansea High Street service on 16th April 1960. The Avan is shining near the centre. (D.K.Jones)

90.   A better view of the buildings was obtained on 13th August 1962 as 0-6-0PT no. 6435 worked the 11.25am from Bridgend. Termination of such trains here ceased on 3rd December 1962, when single car DMUs took over and they continued to Treherbert. (L.W.Rowe)

91. The buildings have gone, staffing ceasing when the location became a request stop on 20th September 1965. The loading gauge is evidence of local goods traffic. There was a siding with a cattle pen, but service was withdrawn in October 1941. (P.J.Garland/R.S.Carpenter coll.)

92. The tunnel was blocked up at each end following its closure, but its construction plaque was treasured and conserved nearby. There were no ventilation shafts, as the terrain above was too thick. (M.Dart coll.)

93.　　The 4.53pm Swansea to Treherbert is about to cross the viaduct in the background on 2nd September 1959 and is at the point where the two routes are closest. (S.P.Derek)

94.　　The Abergwynfi branch is in the foreground, as an 0-6-2T hauls the 5.40pm Treherbert to Neath over the 115yd long Croeserw Viaduct on the same day. (S.P.Derek)

95.   No. 8740 is hauling coal from Abergwynfi on 27th September 1960 and is seen from the disused ex-R&SB track which had been closed for three months by that time. The closure eliminated one viaduct and Gelli Tunnel (167yds), right in the next picture. (R.M.Casserley)

96.   We see no. 8740 moments later. The Abergwynfi line had served Gelli Mill Colliery, until 1894, and Glenavon Colliery, until 1947. (R.M.Casserley)

CYMMER AFAN

Cymmer Afan	1923	1931	1938
Passenger tickets issued	107664	86373	51731
Season tickets issued	139	555	133
Parcels forwarded	3636	1939	2156
General goods forwarded (tons)	308	54	67
Coal and coke received (tons)	10768	1379	-
Other minerals received (tons)	1389	605	1152
General goods received (tons)	15371	9738	15242
Coal and Coke handled	30116	3998	273054
Trucks of livestock handled	-	-	-

XXVI. Cymmer Tunnel is shown with a bold line, the L&OR opening it to goods in 1878 and passengers on 16th July 1880. The South Wales Mineral Railway (left to top) came into use for freight on 10th March 1863. The lines were linked across the valley on the viaduct in 1878 and the L&OR became GWR property in 1883. The line east to Abergwynfi was opened by the latter on 22nd March 1886, the same day as the R&SBR line shown above it. It had opened its line from the west (from Aberavon West Junction) on 2nd November 1885. There was a station at the north end of the viaduct for the Glyncorrwg service from 1918 to 1930 and it was called Cymmer Corrwg from 17th September 1926. By 1929, it had two trains on Fridays and one on Saturdays, plus trains for miners, which had started in about 1880. Inset is the Railway Clearing House diagram of 1905. The R&SBR station was called Afan from 1926.

97. This is the R&SBR station from the west in about 1910. The GWR station was parallel to it, to the south, and linked to it by the footbridge. Staff for these two stations and the next one totalled 29 in 1923 and 17 in 1933. (Lens of Sutton coll.)

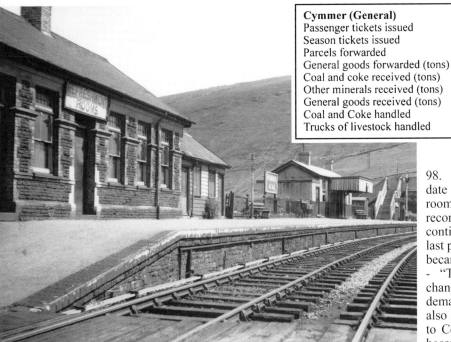

Cymmer (General)	1923	1931	1938
Passenger tickets issued	153919	137245	97639
Season tickets issued	165	107	62
Parcels forwarded	14226	5639	7364
General goods forwarded (tons)	498	601	364
Coal and coke received (tons)	2228	1343	122
Other minerals received (tons)	2543	1818	1217
General goods received (tons)	5985	6760	6320
Coal and Coke handled	1751	15271	96570
Trucks of livestock handled	7	25	-

98. The opening date of the refreshment rooms has not been recorded, but their use continued long after the last passenger had left. It became the village pub - "The Refresh". The changing of trains could demand long waits and also some stiff climbing to Corrwg station. Afan became a request stop in 1965. (R.M.Casserley)

99. Looking in the other direction on 4th January 1958 we have the ex-R&SBR signal box centre and the former GWR one on the left, with the viaduct in the mist. The exchange sidings are on the left. (H.C.Casserley)

100. An up goods train stands at the ex-GWR platform, which was called Cymmer General from 1st July 1924. In the background is the 11.25 Treherbert to Swansea DMU on 27th August 1959. (S.P.Derek)

101. A freight train is on the viaduct in this view from 27th September 1960. New signals have appeared and the platform on the left had been termed a bay since January 1950. Closure of the two signal boxes and their replacement by one with a flat roof (centre) took place on 17th June 1960, as did the closure of the up platform (right and devoid of track). The down one has become an island. (H.C.Casserley)

102. Our final view west includes the 51-lever signal box, which was dismantled after closure on 24th August 1970 and moved to Bargoed. The 1960 alterations had meant truncation of the line on the left and the other two converging onto the Abergwynfi line, as far as the deviation noted under the Blaengwynfi map (XXV). The goods yard had a 2-ton crane and closed on 7th June 1965. Trains from Bridgend terminated here until withdrawn on 22nd June 1970, although trains at school times continued until 14th July of that year. (P.J.Garland/ R.S.Carpenter coll.)

DUFFRYN RHONDDA HALT

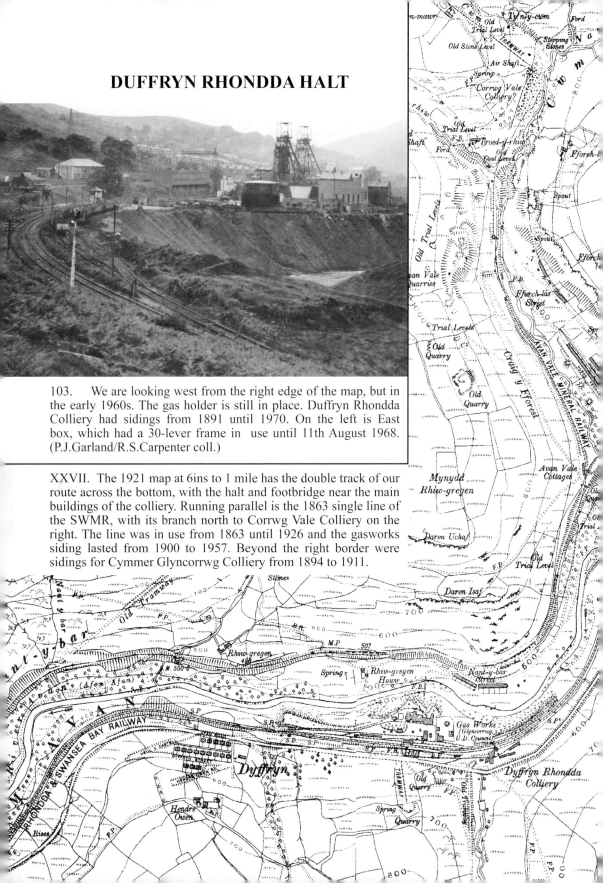

103.   We are looking west from the right edge of the map, but in the early 1960s. The gas holder is still in place. Duffryn Rhondda Colliery had sidings from 1891 until 1970. On the left is East box, which had a 30-lever frame in use until 11th August 1968. (P.J.Garland/R.S.Carpenter coll.)

XXVII. The 1921 map at 6ins to 1 mile has the double track of our route across the bottom, with the halt and footbridge near the main buildings of the colliery. Running parallel is the 1863 single line of the SWMR, with its branch north to Corrwg Vale Colliery on the right. The line was in use from 1863 until 1926 and the gasworks siding lasted from 1900 to 1957. Beyond the right border were sidings for Cymmer Glyncorrwg Colliery from 1894 to 1911.

104.   Another westward view and this features the down platform in about 1965. The halt was in use from 1911 to 1962. In the distance is the 25-lever West box, which was closed on 11th August 1968. (Lens of Sutton coll.)

105.   The up platform and crossover were photographed on 22nd June 1962. Beyond the gate were further colliery sidings, these being in use in 1927-49. (M.Hale)

CYNONVILLE HALT

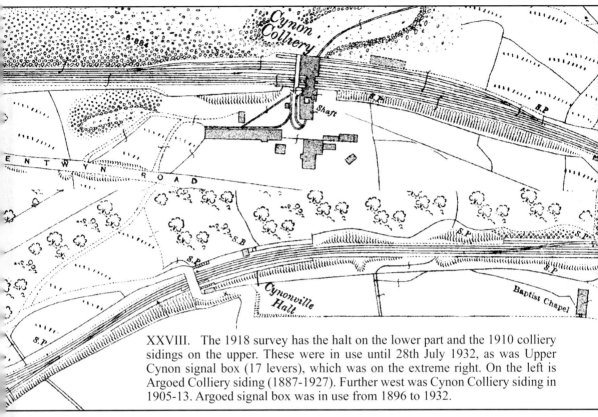

XXVIII. The 1918 survey has the halt on the lower part and the 1910 colliery sidings on the upper. These were in use until 28th July 1932, as was Upper Cynon signal box (17 levers), which was on the extreme right. On the left is Argoed Colliery siding (1887-1927). Further west was Cynon Colliery siding in 1905-13. Argoed signal box was in use from 1896 to 1932.

106.   Opened as Cynon Platform on 10th July 1911, this stop had a chequered history. It closed on 2nd January 1956 and can still be seen, as it is on the Afan Argoed Country Park cycle path. The photograph is from 1962. (M.Hale)

PONTRHYDYFEN

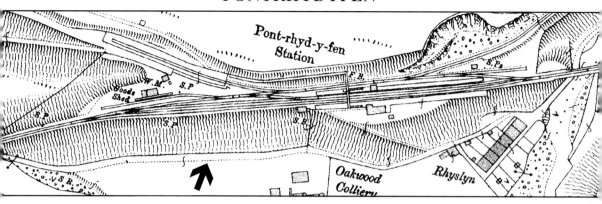

XXIX. The 1918 edition shows the proximity of Oakwood Colliery, but no siding to it. Top left is a private siding, which served Rhydavon Colliery for about 20 years.

107. The station was open from 25th June 1885 to 3rd December 1962. Its goods yard closed on 27th March 1961. The 1.55pm Aberavon Town to Cymmer Afan is departing on 27th September 1960. The curve on the left was completed in 1900 as a link to the SWMR, but never used.
(H.C.Casserley)

108. The 30-lever signal box is behind the camera on the same day. It closed in September 1962 owing to subsidence. The number of men at this station and Cynonville totalled 17 in 1923 and 9 in 1933.
(H.C.Casserley)

CWMAVON (GLAM)

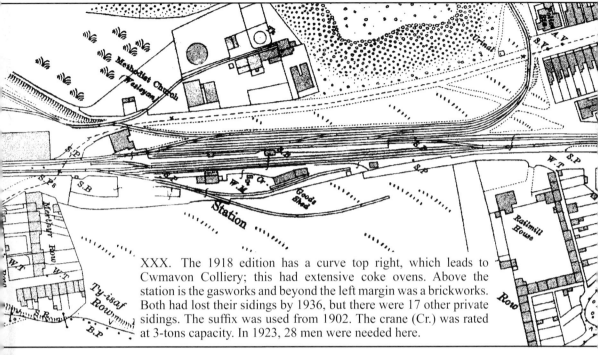

XXX. The 1918 edition has a curve top right, which leads to Cwmavon Colliery; this had extensive coke ovens. Above the station is the gasworks and beyond the left margin was a brickworks. Both had lost their sidings by 1936, but there were 17 other private sidings. The suffix was used from 1902. The crane (Cr.) was rated at 3-tons capacity. In 1923, 28 men were needed here.

109. A train departs up the valley on 27th September 1960. The goods shed is largely obscured by the down side building. Passengers had to walk over the siding, which closed on 2nd November 1964. The signal box in the distance closed on 17th December 1929. Behind the camera was Cwmavon Station box, which had 30 levers and became a ground frame on 10th September 1963. There is now no trace of the station. (R.M.Casserley)

Cwmavon	1923	1931	1938
Passenger tickets issued	155985	75193	42034
Season tickets issued	463	211	165
Parcels forwarded	9784	7848	9995
General goods forwarded (tons)	12474	2766	
Coal and coke received (tons)	3965	2417	
Other minerals received (tons)	15164	3176	
General goods received (tons)	7915	2735	
Coal and Coke handled	11729	3401	
Trucks of livestock handled	18	9	

NORTH OF PORT TALBOT

Pontrhydyfen	1923	1931	1938
Passenger tickets issued	69032	25746	14215
Season tickets issued	204	448	79
Parcels forwarded	2477	1962	3017
General goods forwarded (tons)	291	186	26
Coal and coke received (tons)	1877	389	-
Other minerals received (tons)	573	70	4
General goods received (tons)	1244	305	402
Coal and Coke handled	-	-	236
Trucks of Livestock handles	-	-	-

XXXI. The R&SBR is the straight line running from the top right corner of this 1921 map, which is at 6ins to 1 mile. To the right of it is the River Avan and the curving Port Talbot Railway of 1898. On the left is the R&SBR's Aberavon station and at the bottom is the GWR's General station. Close to it is the PTR's Central station, which received trains from Maesteg, until 1933.

ABERAVON TOWN

XXXII. The 1917 edition has our route from top right to lower left and the GWR between the other corners. The lines cross on the level and not with a bridge, as the map suggests. The goods yard (right) closed on 3rd August 1964; it had a 3-ton crane by 1938, when there were also six private sidings.

110.　　The station was named Aberavon until 1st December 1891, then Aberavon Port Talbot until 1st July 1924, when it became Aberavon Town. In the distance is the R&SBR's two-road engine shed. It was in use from November 1885 until November 1922 and it had 17 engines allocated in 1920. There had earlier been a three-road carriage shed adjacent. The pitched roof was later changed to one with multiple transverse ridges. (Lens of Sutton coll.)

111.　　A poor snap from 29th May 1954 is included as it shows the junction signals, the footbridge and the gates of the level crossing on the A48. The train is an SLS railtour. The number of staff was 53 in 1923 and 37 in 1933. (D.K.Jones coll.)

Aberavon (Town)	1923	1931	1938
Passenger tickets issued	231178	56024	2382
Season tickets issued	603	107	5
Parcels forwarded	8578	5313	4182

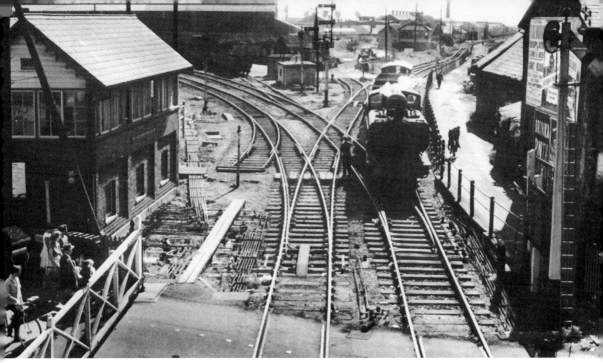

112.   The main road across South Wales is at a standstill on 26th August 1959, while 0-6-0PT no. 9735 brings a few wagons off the single track, which crosses the GWR main line on the level. The two tracks on the left curve to join it. The signal box had four different names and was Port Talbot Aberavon Town when it closed on 19th July 1963. Its 57 levers controlled Plough Junction. In the background is Port Talbot No. 3 Box, which lasted from 1927 to 1963. Beyond it is Mansel Tinplate Works, which had a siding until the line closed on 3rd December 1962. (M.Hale)

113.   The track was doubled northward to Velindre in 1894 and to Cwmavon later. At the end of the platforms is Aberavon Junction for the route to Maesteg. This photograph was taken in about 1960. (Lens of Sutton coll.)

ABERAVON SEASIDE

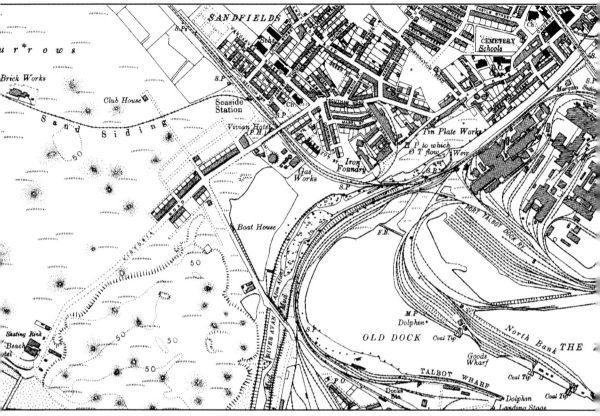

XXXIII. This extract overlaps the left of map XXXI and has Docks station at the bottom. This was the terminus for R&SBR trains between 1891 and 1895, until the line was extended to Swansea. Workmen continued to use the station. The route was also used by freight trains of the Port Talbot Railway & Docks Company running over their own 1898 lines from the Tondu area.

114.   A view northwest in 1955 reveals an unfamiliar flat landscape. The platforms were in use from April 1899 until 3rd December 1962. There was one employee here in the 1930s. In the distance was Baglan Sands Halt from 1st May 1933 to 29th May 1939, but it was closed during its final Winter and was unstaffed. (Stations UK)

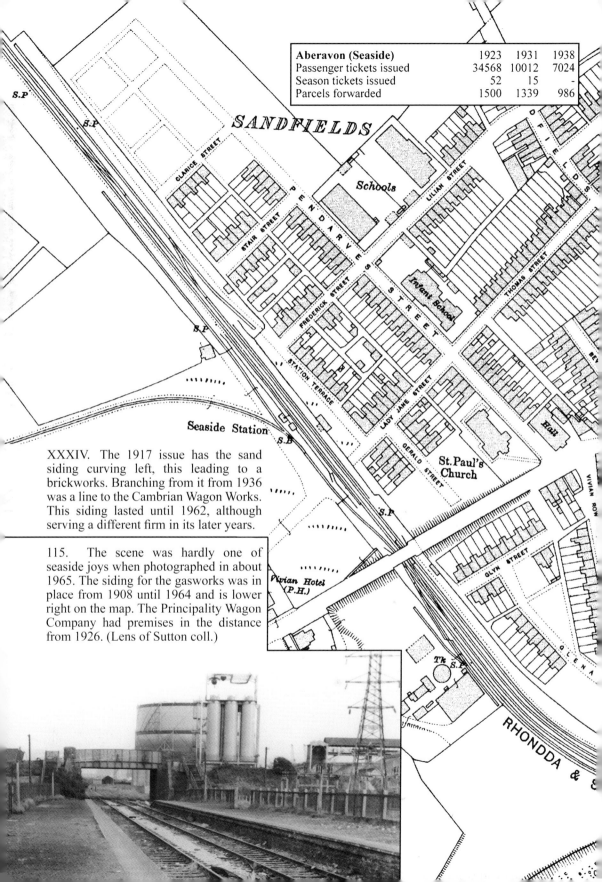

SANDFIELDS

Schools

Infant School

Seaside Station

St. Paul's Church

Vivian Hotel (P.H.)

Aberavon (Seaside)	1923	1931	1938
Passenger tickets issued	34568	10012	7024
Season tickets issued	52	15	-
Parcels forwarded	1500	1339	986

XXXIV. The 1917 issue has the sand siding curving left, this leading to a brickworks. Branching from it from 1936 was a line to the Cambrian Wagon Works. This siding lasted until 1962, although serving a different firm in its later years.

115.　The scene was hardly one of seaside joys when photographed in about 1965. The siding for the gasworks was in place from 1908 until 1964 and is lower right on the map. The Principality Wagon Company had premises in the distance from 1926. (Lens of Sutton coll.)

RHONDDA & S

PORT TALBOT
GENERAL

116. The suffix was used from July 1924 until June 1965. "Parkway" was added in December 1984. This 1955 view east includes a retired clerestory coach.
(Stations UK)

117. New platforms were completed to the north of the earlier ones in 1961 and are seen in the next two pictures. These and the final two are from 13th April 1962 and are intended to show main line traffic, when Avan Valley steam was in terminal decline. This one shows ex-LMS 2-6-4T no. 42182 with chemical tanks near to it and the curve to our route in the background. The other end of it is in picture 112.
(B.W.L.Brooksbank)

118. Westbound with empties is 2-8-0T no. 4284. The old station's facing platforms were replaced by an island one.
(B.W.L.Brooksbank)

119. We finish with two views east from the footbridge. This one includes the goods shed, which remained in use until March 1981. On the level crossing is 4-6-0 "Castle" class no. 5080 *Defiant,* with an express from Paddington to West Wales. (B.W.L.Brooksbank)

Other views can be seen in pictures 82 to 86 in our *Cardiff to Swansea* **album**.

120. No visit to Port Talbot would be complete without sight of its massive steel works. On the right is the signalling centre, which came into use on 22nd September 1963. A new panel was installed in April 2007. No. 5013 *Abergavenny Castle* is braking a Manchester to Swansea train. A wide range of destinations is still on offer from this busy station. (B.W.L.Brooksbank)

MP Middleton Press

EVOLVING THE ULTIMATE RAIL ENCYCLOPEDIA

Easebourne Lane, Midhurst, West Sussex.
GU29 9AZ   Tel:01730 813169

www.middletonpress.co.uk   email:info@middletonpress.co.uk
A-978 0 906520 B- 978 1 873793 C-978 1 901706 D-978 1 904474 E- 978 1 906008

All titles listed below were in print at time of publication - please check current availability by looking at our website - *www.middletonpress.co.uk* or by requesting a Brochure which includes our *LATEST* RAILWAY TITLES also our TRAMWAY, TROLLEYBUS, MILITARY and WATERWAYS series

A
Abergavenny to Merthyr C 91 8
Abertillery and Ebbw Vale Lines D 84 5
Allhallows - Branch Line to A 62 8
Alton - Branch Lines to A 11 6
Andover to Southampton A 82 6
Ascot - Branch Lines around A 64 2
Ashburton - Branch Line to B 95 4
Ashford - Steam to Eurostar B 67 1
Ashford to Dover A 48 2
Austrian Narrow Gauge D 04 3
Avonmouth - BL around D 42 5
Aylesbury to Rugby D 91 3

B
Baker Street to Uxbridge D 90 6
Banbury to Birmingham D 27 2
Banbury to Cheltenham E 63 5
Bangor to Portmadoc E 72 7
Barking to Southend C 80 2
Barmouth to Pwllheli E 53 6
Barry - Branch Lines around D 50 0
Bath Green Park to Bristol C 36 9
Bath to Evercreech Junction A 60 4
Bedford to Wellingborough D 31 9
Birmingham to Wolverhampton E 25 3
Bletchley to Cambridge D 94 4
Bletchley to Rugby E 07 9
Bodmin - Branch Lines around B 83 1
Bournemouth & Poole Trys B 47 3
Bournemouth to Evercreech Jn A 46 8
Bournemouth to Weymouth A 57 4
Brecon to Neath D 43 2
Brecon to Newport D 16 6
Brecon to Newtown E 06 2
Brighton to Eastbourne A 16 1
Brighton to Worthing A 03 1
Bromley South to Rochester B 23 7
Bromsgrove to Birmingham D 87 6
Bromsgrove to Gloucester D 73 9
Brunel - A railtour of his achievements D 74 6
Bude - Branch Line to B 29 9
Burnham to Evercreech Junction B 68 0

C
Cambridge to Ely D 55 5
Canterbury - Branch Lines around B 58 9
Cardiff to Dowlais (Cae Harris) E 47 5
Cardiff to Swansea E 42 0
Carlisle to Hawick E 85 7
Carmarthen to Fishguard E 66 6
Caterham & Tattenham Corner B 25 1
Chard and Yeovil - BLs around C 30 7
Charing Cross to Dartford A 75 8
Charing Cross to Orpington A 96 3
Cheddar - Branch Line to B 90 9
Cheltenham to Andover C 43 7
Cheltenham to Redditch D 81 4
Chichester to Portsmouth A 14 7
Clapham Junction to Beckenham Jn B 36 7
Cleobury Mortimer - BLs around E 18 5
Clevedon & Portishead - BLs to D 18 0
Colonel Stephens D 62 3
Consett to South Shields E 57 4
Cornwall Narrow Gauge D 56 2
Corris and Vale of Rheidol E 65 9
Craven Arms to Llandeilo E 35 2
Craven Arms to Wellington E 33 8
Crawley to Littlehampton A 34 5
Cromer - Branch Lines around C 26 0
Croydon to East Grinstead B 48 0
Crystal Palace and Catford Loop B 87 1
Cyprus Narrow Gauge E 13 0

D
Darlington - Leamside - Newcastle E 28 4
Darlington to Newcastle D 98 2
Dartford to Sittingbourne B 34 3
Derwent Valley - Branch Line to the D 06 7
Devon Narrow Gauge E 09 3
Didcot to Banbury D 02 9
Didcot to Swindon C 84 0
Didcot to Winchester C 13 0
Dorset & Somerset Narrow Gauge D 76 0

Douglas - Laxey - Ramsey E 75 8
Douglas to Peel C 88 8
Douglas to Port Erin C 55 0
Douglas to Ramsey D 39 5
Dover to Ramsgate A 78 9
Dublin Northwards in the 1950s E 31 4
Dunstable - Branch Lines to E 27 7

E
Ealing to Slough C 42 0
East Cornwall Mineral Railways D 22 7
East Croydon to Three Bridges A 53 6
Eastern Spain Narrow Gauge E 56 7
East Grinstead - Branch Lines to A 07 9
East London - Branch Lines of C 44 4
East London Line B 80 0
East of Norwich - Branch Lines E 69 7
Effingham Junction - BLs around A 74 1
Ely to Norwich C 90 1
Enfield Town & Palace Gates - BL to D 32 6
Epsom to Horsham A 30 7
Eritrean Narrow Gauge E 38 3
Euston to Harrow & Wealdstone C 89 5
Exeter to Barnstaple B 15 2
Exeter to Newton Abbot C 49 9
Exeter to Tavistock B 69 5
Exmouth - Branch Lines to B 00 8

F
Fairford - Branch Line to A 52 9
Falmouth, Helston & St. Ives - BL to C 74 1
Fareham to Salisbury A 67 3
Faversham to Dover B 05 3
Felixstowe & Aldeburgh - BL to D 20 3
Fenchurch Street to Barking C 20 8
Festiniog - 50 yrs of enterprise C 83 3
Festiniog 1946-55 E 01 7
Festiniog in the Fifties B 68 5
Festiniog in the Sixties B 91 6
Finsbury Park to Alexandra Palace C 02 8
Frome to Bristol B 77 0

G
Gloucester to Bristol D 35 7
Gloucester to Cardiff D 66 1
Gosport - Branch Lines around A 36 9
Greece Narrow Gauge D 72 2

H
Hampshire Narrow Gauge D 36 4
Harrow to Watford D 14 2
Hastings to Ashford A 37 6
Hawkhurst - Branch Line to A 66 6
Hayling - Branch Line to A 12 3
Hay-on-Wye - Branch Lines around D 92 0
Haywards Heath to Seaford A 28 4
Hemel Hempstead - Branch Lines to D 88 3
Henley, Windsor & Marlow - BL to C77 2
Hereford to Newport D 54 8
Hertford and Hatfield - BLs around E 58 1 6
Hertford Loop E 71 0
Hexham to Carlisle D 75 3
Hitchin to Peterborough D 07 4
Holborn Viaduct to Lewisham A 81 9
Horsham - Branch Lines to A 02 4
Huntingdon - Branch Line to A 93 2

I
Ilford to Shenfield C 97 0
Ilfracombe - Branch Line to B 21 3
Industrial Rlys of the South East A 09 3
Ipswich to Saxmundham C 41 3
Isle of Wight Lines - 50 yrs C 12 3

K
Kent Narrow Gauge C 45 1
Kidderminster to Shrewsbury E 10 9
Kingsbridge - Branch Line to C 98 7
Kings Cross to Potters Bar E 62 8
Kingston & Hounslow Loops A 83 3
Kingswear - Branch Line to C 17 8

L
Lambourn - Branch Line to C 70 3
Launceston & Princetown - BL to C 19 2
Lewisham to Dartford A 92 5
Lines around Wimbledon B 75 6

Liverpool Street to Chingford D 01 2
Liverpool Street to Ilford C 34 5
Llandeilo to Swansea E 46 8
London Bridge to Addiscombe B 20 6
London Bridge to East Croydon A 58 1
Longmoor - Branch Lines to A 41 3
Looe - Branch Line to C 22 2
Lowestoft - Branch Lines around E 40 6
Ludlow to Hereford E 14 7
Lydney - Branch Lines around E 26 0
Lyme Regis - Branch Line to A 45 1
Lynton - Branch Line to B 04 6

M
Machynlleth to Barmouth E 54 3
March - Branch Lines around B 09 1
Marylebone to Rickmansworth D 49 4
Melton Constable to Yarmouth Beach E 03 1
Mexborough to Swinton E 36 9
Midhurst - Branch Lines around A 49 9
Midhurst - Branch Lines of E 78 9
Mitcham Junction Lines B 01 5
Mitchell & company C 59 8
Monmouth - Branch Lines to E 20 8
Monmouthshire Eastern Valleys D 71 5
Moretonhampstead - BL to C 27 7
Moreton-in-Marsh to Worcester D 26 5
Mountain Ash to Neath D 80 7

N
Newbury to Westbury C 66 6
Newcastle to Hexham D 69 2
Newport (IOW) - Branch Lines to A 26 0
Newquay - Branch Lines to C 71 0
Newton Abbot to Plymouth C 60 4
Newtown to Aberystwyth E 41 3
North East German Narrow Gauge D 44 9
Northern France Narrow Gauge C 75 8
Northern Spain Narrow Gauge E 83 3
North London Line B 94 7
North Woolwich - BLs around C 65 9

O
Ongar - Branch Line to E 05 5
Oswestry - Branch Lines around E 60 4
Oswestry to Whitchurch E 81 9
Oxford to Bletchley D 57 9
Oxford to Moreton-in-Marsh D 15 9

P
Paddington to Ealing C 37 6
Paddington to Princes Risborough C 81 9
Padstow - Branch Line to B 54 1
Peterborough to Kings Lynn E 32 1
Plymouth - BLs around B 98 5
Plymouth to St. Austell C 63 5
Pontypool to Mountain Ash D 65 4
Pontypridd to Port Talbot E 86 4
Porthmadog 1954-94 - BL around B 31 2
Portmadoc 1923-46 - BL around B 13 8
Portsmouth to Southampton A 31 4
Portugal Narrow Gauge E 67 3
Potters Bar to Cambridge D 70 8
Princes Risborough - Branch Lines to D 05 0
Princes Risborough to Banbury C 85 7

R
Reading to Basingstoke B 27 5
Reading to Didcot C 79 6
Reading to Guildford A 47 5
Redhill to Ashford A 73 4
Return to Blaenau 1970-82 C 64 2
Rhymney and New Tredegar Lines E 48 2
Rickmansworth to Aylesbury D 61 6
Romania & Bulgaria Narrow Gauge E 23 9
Romneyrail C 32 1
Ross-on-Wye - Branch Lines around E 30 7
Ruabon to Barmouth E 84 0
Rugby to Birmingham E 37 6
Ryde to Ventnor A 19 2

S
Salisbury to Westbury B 39 8
Saxmundham to Yarmouth C 69 7
Saxony Narrow Gauge D 47 0
Seaton & Sidmouth - Branch Lines to A 95 6

Selsey - Branch Line to A 04 8
Sheerness - Branch Line to B 16 2
Shrewsbury - Branch Line to B 86 4
Shrewsbury to Chester E 70 3
Shrewsbury to Ludlow E 21 5
Shrewsbury to Newtown E 29 1
Sierra Leone Narrow Gauge D 28 9
Sirhowy Valley Line E 12 3
Sittingbourne to Ramsgate A 90 1
Slough to Newbury C 56 7
South African Two-foot gauge E 51 2
Southampton to Bournemouth A 42 0
Southend & Southminster - B Ls to E 76 5
Southern France Narrow Gauge C 47 5
South London Line B 46 6
Southwold - Branch Line to A 15 4
Spalding - Branch Lines around E 52 9
St Albans to Bedford D 08 1
St. Austell to Penzance C 67 3
Steaming through the Isle of Wight A 56 7
Steaming through West Hants A 69 7
Stourbridge to Wolverhampton E 16 1
St. Pancras to Barking D 68 5
St. Pancras to St. Albans C 78 9
Stratford-upon-Avon to Birmingham D 77 7
Stratford-upon-Avon to Cheltenham C 25 3
Surrey Narrow Gauge C 87 1
Sussex Narrow Gauge C 68 0
Swanley to Ashford B 45 9
Swansea to Carmarthen E 59 8
Swindon to Bristol C 96 3
Swindon to Gloucester D 46 3
Swindon to Newport D 30 2
Swiss Narrow Gauge C 94 9

T
Talyllyn - 50 years C 39 0
Taunton to Barnstaple B 60 2
Taunton to Exeter C 82 6
Tavistock to Plymouth B 88 6
Tenterden - Branch Line to A 21 5
Three Bridges to Brighton A 35 2
Tilbury Loop C 86 4
Tiverton - Branch Lines around C 62 8
Tivetshall to Beccles D 41 8
Tonbridge to Hastings A 44 4
Torrington - Branch Lines to B 37 4
Towcester - Branch Lines around E 39 0
Tunbridge Wells - Branch Lines to A 32 1

U
Upwell - Branch Line to B 64 0

V
Victoria to Bromley South A 98 7
Vivarais Revisited E 08 6

W
Wantage - Branch Line to D 25 8
Wareham to Swanage - 50 yrs D 09 8
Waterloo to Windsor A 54 3
Waterloo to Woking A 38 3
Watford to Leighton Buzzard D 45 6
Welshpool to Llanfair E 49 9
Wenford Bridge to Fowey C 09 3
Westbury to Bath B 55 8
Westbury to Taunton C 76 5
West Cornwall Mineral Railways D 48 7
West Croydon to Epsom B 08 4
West German Narrow Gauge D 93 7
West London - Branch Lines of C 50 5
West London Line B 84 8
West Wiltshire - Branch Lines of D 12 8
Weymouth - Branch Lines around A 65 9
Willesden Junction to Richmond B 71 8
Wimbledon to Beckenham C 58 1
Wimbledon to Epsom B 62 6
Wimborne - Branch Lines around A 97 0
Wisbech 1800-1901 C 93 2
Wisbech - Branch Lines around C 01 7
Witham & Kelvedon - BLs around E 82 6
Woking to Alton A 59 8
Woking to Portsmouth A 25 3
Woking to Southampton A 55 0
Wolverhampton to Shrewsbury E 44 4
Worcester to Birmingham D 97 5
Worcester to Hereford D 38 8
Worthing to Chichester A 06 2

Y
Yeovil - 50 yrs change C 38 3
Yeovil to Dorchester A 76 5
Yeovil to Exeter A 91 8